Copyright @2023 by Demeter North

All rights reserved. No part of this book may be reproduced in any form or by any electronic or mechanical means, including information storage and retrieval systems, without permission in writing from the publisher, except by reviewers, who may quote brief passages in a review.

This publication contains the opinions and ideas of its author. It is intended to provide helpful and informative material on the subjects addressed in the publication. The author and publisher specifically disclaim all responsibility for any liability, loss or risk, personal or otherwise, which is incurred as a consequence, directly or indirectly, of the use and application of any of the contents of this book.

WORKBOOK PRESS LLC
187 E Warm Springs Rd,
Suite B285, Las Vegas, NV 89119, USA

| | |
|---|---|
| Website: | https://workbookpress.com/ |
| Hotline: | 1-888-818-4856 |
| Email: | admin@workbookpress.com |

Ordering Information:
Quantity sales. Special discounts are available on quantity purchases by corporations, associations, and others. For details, contact the publisher at the address above.

Library of Congress Control Number:

ISBN-13:    978-1-960752-44-4 (Paperback Version)
            978-1-960752-45-1 (Digital Version)

REV. DATE: 02/27/2023

# TABLE OF CONTENTS

| | |
|---|---|
| Intro | 1 |
| Chapter 1 | 3 |
| Chapter 2 | 19 |
| Chapter 3 | 36 |
| Chapter 4 | 49 |
| Chapter 5 | 66 |
| Chapter 6 | 82 |
| Chapter 7 | 100 |
| Chapter 8 | 123 |
| Chapter 9 | 144 |
| Chapter 10 | 168 |
| Chapter 11 | 189 |
| Chapter 12 | 207 |
| Chapter 13 | 227 |
| Chapter 14 | 242 |
| The Glossary | 255 |
| In Acknowledgement | 259 |

# SURVIVING HELL

## TRIP TO IRAQ

DEMETER NORTH

# INTRO

    This story is about several average American kids who, like all service members sent into combat, have to grow up all too fast. They come from the city, country and suburbs. Backgrounds range from rich parents, to trying to escape a life of drug, stealing, and family abuse. These are fathers, brothers and sons. Some support family overseas and from other countries, trying to give them a better life. Some are on their own, disowned from their families. They come from every walk of life. They are from every religion to no religion at all—every background and culture. No two have the same story, nor are their experiences the same. Yet they all seem to bond and work together as if they knew each other all their lives. Nowhere else would you find better brothers who would be willing to sacrifice everything for one another. This story is written in a manner that gives justice to the service members it is about. The story is intentional to the character of the writer and the Marines they are about.

# CHAPTER 1

It was April 2004 and my first deployment to Iraq after what felt like thousands of hours of training. My Squad had been with me since the beginning of boot camp and my best friend was Chap. There was also Jonathan and Dave, who were best friends. The four of us did everything together. We volunteered for this deployment so we could continue to be in the same unit. We thought there was nothing we could not accomplish together and had a blast doing whatever it was. A brotherhood forms when you go through boot camp and it creates the need to watch out for one another. These were my battle buddies and this experience would bond us and bring us together like nothing we've ever been through.

Our journey began on a long C-130 (large cargo and passenger plane) ride. We had loaded up in full gear the only thing missing was ammunition and they do not let you carry that due to flying. Everyone always felt secure and invincible wearing full gear and that made the trip feel a little better despite our lack of ammo. We weren't carrying much, only what we could fit on our bodies. Most of our gear was being transported in a quad con and delivered to the base. Our combat load along with a select few knickknacks we could sneak in were all that went with us.

I looked over to Dave across from me and I could tell he was excited. All he talked about was how he couldn't wait to land and be fully loaded with grenades and rounds for his M249 SAW (light machine gun). He was anxious to go to combat and make a difference; he was a Patriot through and through. He felt everyone should join and do their part out of duty for our country. He was here to be a hero at least that's what he believed.

Jonathan was sitting to my right his mood was different sort of quiet. I saw him praying several times as the C-130 jumped in turbulence. He needed some extra money to send to his wife and daughter back home. He had no notions of glory or fame; he was here because he had to be. The combat pay wasn't a big boost but it was more than enough to get them out of debt and back on their feet again. The money was tax free and a bonus for them to put into savings or maybe even take that honeymoon they never had.

Chap, my buddy and partner in crime, we were bonded in boot camp. He had all the traits I lacked especially that survival instinct to keep me out of trouble. I had the charisma to bring people together and do things they normally don't try. We found out pretty fast that we made quite the team and together things were never boring and just seemed to always work out. He was here because I was here. When I told him I volunteered he said, "Now what the hell did you do that for now I got to go to keep you alive." Sure enough that same day he volunteered and here we are on the C-130.

I am here because Jonathan got the orders to go and well I could let him go alone. It didn't take much to convince Dave to go with us. I knew Chap would go as soon as he heard I was going and of course there was no way he would let me go without him.

Well, as for me, I was the friend most families warn their kids about. I was that bad influence that had really bad Ideas that makes everyone have a lot of fun, and yet get into so much trouble. I was the guy that everyone came to when they wanted to have fun, but everyone avoided when there was work to be done. I believe in working as hard as I play. I was always looking for a good time constantly and was overly social; at least that is how I was before deployment.

On the C-130, heading into God knows what; I was feeling anxious and curious. I was thinking what would it be like? Would I be brave or would I be the guy who got scared and cowered? Would I get shot? Would I make it back alive? Turbulence distracted my thoughts and you could see sky through the side panels when it bumped.

As the plane started banking for a landing the ride got real rough. I could feel myself getting nauseous and I asked Chap for a puke bag. He smirked as he tossed the bag to the back of the C-130. Not being able to hold it any more I threw up in my helmet. It was that or all over me and the floor. I knew we weren't changing clothes any time soon so my options were splatter on me and the folks next to me or the helmet. Everyone laughed at me when they should have been glad I chose my helmet. I know it was more of a nervous take your mind off of what is going on kind of laughter so I ignored it and gave them a little more distraction by calling Chap a few choice names and left it at that. I would get him back later though.

The C-130 landed with just a few bumps. You could feel the change in the air when the door opened. I went to step out and "POW" the heat and dry air hit my lungs. I thought

I was suffocating for a second as the good air in my lungs got replaced with 130 degree moisture stealing demon breath! Once we were on the ground and out of the C-130s way so it could leave us, I used the remaining water in my canteen to clean out my helmet. I smelled it to make sure it would not gag me and strapped it on. The rest of our gear was on a separate C-130 and would be delivered later. We continued walking on the tarmac to our designated spot when we heard a siren and weren't sure what was going on.

That's when we heard it for the first time, a sound that even today when anything makes it, makes me flinch. A light air sound, it's like the sound of a whistling nerf ball if it were 10 times the size. Then the impact not even 100 yards away, dirt and debris flies everywhere and you can feel the compression in your chest even at that distance. Most of us weren't sure what to do just standing there looking for guidance. We had no ammo, we couldn't shoot back, the only cover was the C-130 and we were pretty sure it was what they were trying to hit.

All we could think was, damn! There's nowhere to go! We are sitting ducks! We need some ammo we can't shoot back! We have no cover! The split "millisecond" moment is over and we split up into our squads. We put 50 yards between each group so that damage done to the unit could be minimalized. We got into circles and surrounded ourselves with what gear we had. There wasn't much to do at that point but start smoking and wait for our convoy to pick us up. It should have been here already. Why it wasn't here already was anybody's guess. What is taking so long? Waiting is a painful thing for the mind.

We could hear guns, giant nerf whistle sounds, and explosions but it wasn't close so we had no idea what was going on. The C-130 had now taken off and left us. Now we were the only thing out in the open, vulnerable to whatever without our ammo. Every so often a few more nerf whistling mortar rounds would come in and we would all cringe and wait to be hit. The impact would be about 100 yards, 80 yards, 120 yards. We wondered if they were actually trying to hit us or did they just have no clue as to how close they were getting. After about a dozen rounds or so, and seeing their horrible accuracy, I told my squad, "Relax they can't hit the broad side of a barn, let's get some rest while we can."

Dave asked for a smoke and I gave him one. He, in turn, handed it to Jonathan whose hands were shaking. I think the mortars rattled him a little so I gave Dave another smoke and nodded to him acknowledging I had noticed Jonathan shaking. Chap pulled out some dip and started spitting in his spare canteen. We just sat there taking in all the sounds trying to imagine what it looked like up close. We could hear every shot and explosion but couldn't see anything except when a mortar came our way and landed close.

After an hour or so the fighting seemed to have stopped as we hadn't heard the mortar fire or shooting in a while. Someone shouted and we could see the convoy coming in the distance. Everyone was thinking it was about time. We were all so angry that they were late and wanted to yell a few choice words until we saw the condition the convoy was in. You could see the damage even from a distance. You could tell they had gone through a rough fight. Several of the vehicles had heavy impact damage and you could see where the mechanics had made emergency repairs to get the vehicles going again. We could see a few had blood on them, none seemed seriously wounded but we noticed they were under manned. The fact that they were short people wasn't a good sign.

They slowly got out and pulled MRE's (Meals Ready To Eat) and water out of their trucks and started passing them around. As much as I didn't like MRE's I hadn't eaten in 10 hours and was hungry and thanked God for the water, I had to use mine earlier on my helmet. That reminds me I owe Chap one. I leaned over and smashed my helmet on his making a loud knock sound. He said a few profanities and kept eating as he knew why I had hit him.

We never asked but they must have been part of that firefight that had taken place earlier and they had taken quite the beating. We assumed that the missing personnel were wounded or worse. It was hard to tell as no one in the convoy wanted to talk about anything. They started handing out ammunition which gave a huge mental boost. It was almost like a wave went through the group. Everyone felt a lot more secure now that we could defend ourselves. Once we were armed they loaded us into the convoy and we headed out.

As we drove through each town there were people on roofs taking pot shots at us. The convoy didn't even slow down when it happened—if anything, they sped up. On the ride to base I studied the Marines escorting us. They seemed different from us, something I'd never seen before. Most, if not all, when you looked at them seemed as if they saw through you like you weren't there. They were doing their job and nothing more. It seemed we were just cargo to them, not human at all. I didn't get why at the time why they would be like that.

It didn't take long before the lead truck spotted what might be an IED (Improvised Explosive Device) and the whole convoy had to stop. We waited as the Marines who had been escorting us went to work. We watched as they were spreading out entering buildings and setting up spotters making sure that the area was clear. Not long after that the IED patrol showed up and sent out their team. It didn't seem to take them long to clear the area and remove the IED.

We wondered what they were doing and how they were doing it but the visibility in the 7 ton (unarmored transport truck) from the back was pretty much just the shooting slot in the side for each passenger. This didn't give us a good view of anything.

We were on our way again and the rest of the drive went without incident. You couldn't help but wonder, "How could anyone live here? How could anything possibly flourish?" There was desert as far as the eye could see. No vegetation, no water source, there was nothing for countless miles as we drove by. It was like a scene from a western movie where the guy is stranded and there's nothing for miles—only this is worse. There are not even any tumble weeds, cactuses, or anything. All I could see is rock and sand. Just rock and sand everywhere.

The convoy passed the first checkpoint and we studied it thankful for something to see other than desert. There were scar marks all over the place from countless firefights and mortar impacts. In the towns after the checkpoint I noticed the buildings were no better, it was almost as if someone took a machine gun to every wall down the street and just let loose on purpose. Bullet holes were in everything. I started to get the feeling this was not going to be at all what we had thought.

I could see the people in the street staring up at the vehicles shouting with their hands up and chasing us. The drivers appeared to have candy and threw it as far as they could. The people ran towards the candy and away from us. At the time I thought, why throw it so far why not just toss it to them nicely? The air smelled as if someone hadn't flushed the toilet in days. The stink seemed to be everywhere going through the town. It was hard to breathe with the hot air and the smell in the back of this truck. We would all be glad to get to our destination.

We pulled up to the final check point of our base station in Ramadi. It was almost as if a miracle had touched this place. There were plants, gardens, animals, and farms everywhere. I saw a few dogs here and there, though they looked diseased and malnourished. Then I realized why there seemed to be life here—we were right by the river. The farmers and locals were using its water source to supply the land with much needed moisture to grow and survive. As beautiful as the scenery was, it didn't change the fact that the heat radiated out in waves of what felt like dragon's breath. It would take us a bit to get used to this water robbing heat.

We entered the base, unloaded the trucks, and were escorted to our new quarters. They were run down bunk houses the Iraqi soldiers had been using when they occupied the base. We were assigned a bunk house (living area). Chap took the bottom bunk and I took the top. We wanted to stay together and it took some trading of goods to convince two guys to switch out with Dave and Jonathan so they could be together as well.

I didn't really want the candy bars I brought anyway. I figured the heat already ruined them, so losing them to have my friends together was no sacrifice at all. Dave and Jonathan wrestled over who got top bunk and Jonathan won. I think Dave let him; he still seemed concerned that he was shaking earlier. But Jonathan's nerves seemed to be fine now.

So we are here and settled in our spots. It wasn't much but it was going to be livable. There was an air conditioning unit but it looked like it hadn't worked in a long time. We will have to fix that. We surveyed and saw that the guys who stayed here before left us a TV. Now all we need is to acquire a DVD player or game console.

We were going to have to come up with some ideas to make this place more comfortable. We are going to be bored to death if we don't find something to entertain us; either that or we will be at the gym 24/7.

We unpacked all our gear when it had finally arrived. I had snuck in several posters and a radio. I thought the radio was great until it turned out to be useless, nothing but mosque music, some guy preaching and singing at the same time and a prayer going on and on. The posters however worked nice to distract you from the look of the place. This was going to be our home for six to eight months. The more we had to distract us the more bearable it was going to be.

# CHAPTER 2

Chap and I had been assigned our duties for post. The missions we would be going on would work around the dates and times of those duties. I had been assigned the front gate tower on the right side. My shift was 12:00 am to 2:00 pm Monday, Wednesday, and Fridays. Chap got the tower next to me on the right it was about 30 yards down and the exact same shift. Dave and Jonathan however weren't so lucky. Dave got the back gate tower and a completely different shift 2:00 pm to 4:00 am Monday, Wednesday, and Fridays.

Jonathan's shift was 12:00 am to 2:00 pm Tuesday, Thursday, and Saturday. Hanging out on our off time was only going to be on Sundays with our schedules so different. That is if we do not have a mission to go on. We were all pretty disappointed about that. We were getting hungry and noticed it was time to eat. We were looking forward to some real food. As we walked to the Chow Hall (Dinning hall) we noticed the buildings were damaged all on the outside and had been repaired multiple times. Impacts riddled the ground and made it fairly uneven except where the sand was.

We heard a light shwooo sound and just as Chap was turning to ask me what that was it exploded on the building across from us. Reacting instantly Chap and I both hit the ground and looked at each other and started laughing. We weren't laughing because it was funny. It was more of an adrenaline rush of a "holy crap that was close could you believe that just happened" laugh. I found humor to fix most situations we came across; otherwise you could end up going crazy. We brushed the sand off each other's backs and continued going to chow.

The Chow Hall wasn't that big but they had it set up very well. They had a lot of food options. There was a buffet people were lining up at. It had salads, meats, sandwiches, fruits, yogurts, breads, soups. It was like a typical buffet place but way better. As Chap and I continued on in we could smell something wonderful, our heads turned to the delicious aromas and we spotted the main lunch line. They had steaks cooking and were smothering mushrooms and onions for people. Our jaws dropped and we almost couldn't believe it but our noses told us it was real!

Keeping the Marines on base happy was obviously very important. For most men like me food is the way to their heart. Chap and I both felt the love. Chap looked at me and said, "Dude we found our new slice of heaven." I nodded in agreement. I made a salad with what you would call everything except the kitchen sink this included chopping up the steak I waited in line for. Chap had a steak, a few sandwiches, yogurt and several different fruits. This was the best we had eaten since joining the military. The Chow Hall back home is okay but this was a novelty, like we're all someone special and getting the royal treatment!

As Chap and I finished up dinner I told him to grab a few of those raw potatoes before we walked out. Of course he gave me the odd "what are you crazy?" look, so I showed him that I stuffed a few in my pockets. Shaking his head, he didn't argue and filled his pockets as well. On our way back to the bunks Chap, dreading another one of my schemes, finally got up the nerve to ask what I planned on doing with raw potatoes. I responded, "Just wait till I'm done then complain about what I'm doing or help me out more next time." Chap laughed lowly as to say I know you're up to something I won't approve of.

We were two tired guys, and we knew we needed sleep before our shift duties. Chap and I tried, but every four hours the mosque played prayer music which bellows across the base and vibrates your eardrums. Of course this just has to begin right when we lay down in our bunks. Two hours into our sleep came the next interruption. It was around 11:00 pm, right before our shifts. Mortars came raining in hitting the base. The sirens are wailing and with the thoom of impacts. No more sleep for us. We decided it was time to get up and just head to our posts, since there wasn't enough time to catch anymore sleep and be able to wake up in time for duty.

Standing watch for the first time was eye opening from what we thought it was going to be like, compared to what it actually was like. I had figured we would be bored out of our minds staring at scenery that never changed and would need to find something for my mind to do to stay sharp. I planned accordingly and prepared myself for the job. Spotting movement should have been easy, we would be high up, have lots of gear for the task at hand, energy drinks for when I got tired, and a few snacks to keep me from starving. I could read a book, and practice some training to occupy my mind in-between. I thought I was ready.

When I got to my Post, the Marine on duty with me was half way through his shift and looked pretty tired. I barely rated a glance from him. He didn't know me and didn't want to get to know me based on his demeanor for reasons of his own. I could see his gear was fairly rattled with rips, tears and a few stains. When I took a good look at his face it was scarred but I wasn't sure if it was from Iraq or something before. I could see the bullet holes all inside the tower from countless fire fights. There was a cigarette butt can and it was almost full. Everyone must smoke during the day shifts because you didn't dare do it in the open at night.

It was pitch black and I couldn't see anything except through my night vision goggles. The terrain in front of the tower was covered with farmer's fields, trees, ravines and a river that could be crossed by boat on the left. In my mind I saw hundreds of places our enemies could hide and use as cover to get close to the base. The spotting towers were in charge of finding any threat and protecting this base and all those within. Spotting something at night in enough time is almost impossible with all the hiding places factored together. I couldn't smoke or I would make my face a snipers target with the glow of the cigarette. I couldn't see in the tower to read or do anything because it needed to be so dark no one could see where I was standing if they were looking at the tower. I was wired up pretty tight trying to do and think of it all. I couldn't afford to make a mistake, people are depending on me.

As I was looking out the firing window I realized I was nothing but a target and started to get a little paranoid. Now I was checking everything and every piece of movement with my night vision goggles. I was zooming in on bushes, looking at the rooftops on the houses, checking the dips in the ravines. Being a target meant I had to see them first before they could see me. Several hours went by while I was trying to be over vigilant. I was starting to wear down. My attention span was reaching its limit and I was starting to feel bone tired at this point. I had slept only 2 hours and it wasn't even a good sleep.

I guess I was making the Marine with me nervous because he started my way and said, "Relax, this must be your first time out here, my names Jeff. There's no point in working yourself up over what might be out there. It either is or isn't. Just stay away from the middle of the tower window." I could tell Jeff had been through quite a bit, I wanted to ask him lots of questions but the way Jeff acted I knew I wasn't going to get the answers I wanted if, I got any answers at all. So, I tried to be more nonchalant and unwind yet stay alert.

I was about to open my energy drink to give me a boost when Jeff said, "Movement one hundred and fifty yards weapon up stay alert. My adrenalin kicked into high gear, I put down the energy drink that I hadn't even opened and went to look where Jeff was pointing with my night vision. I thought I saw something but I wasn't completely sure. I radioed to the front gate to ask if they could verify the movement. They responded to us saying it's just a wild dog going through the bushes in front of the post. I was a little disappointed—it had me on the edge of my seat with my trigger finger ready and safety off.

I had an adrenalin rush with no action to release it. Jeff looked at me and laughed and said, "You're going to go crazy out here if you keep jumping at everything. Your time will come devil pup, just relax. Remember it's your reaction to the situation when it happens that matters—nothing before and nothing after. Have a smoke, chill out and sit down for a while."

Just as I began to sit in my chair I heard a POP. Jeff did what looked like a ballerina spin, arms wrapping in one direction as he spun around before dropping to the floor. I shouted a few profanities as I tried shining a light to see where Jeff had been hit so I could stop the bleeding. I tried radioing in but there was too much chatter already on our line—people were engaging and calling in what was happening. I could hear them talking about insurgents spotted, they would call the distance and how many. Several of them kept reporting that they were taking fire and still engaging.

I could hear the machine gun fire from both the towers and from the insurgents they were fighting. I heard a few explosions, but it was hard to tell if it was the towers or the insurgents taking that damage— the echo they had made came from behind me. It almost sounded as if the other towers on the back gate had been hit with an explosive of some sort. With the echo it was hard to tell.

It seemed a long time but was only a split second... I had to check to make sure we were clear. I couldn't abandon my post and take Jeff down stairs, so once I saw all lines of fire were covered in our spot I knew I had to try and save Jeff. I got his flak jacket off to see where he had been hit. It didn't look good, it had missed his Kevlar plating at the top, went into his right upper chest, and out the back of the shoulder. I took my k-bar and tore his sleeves off to make gauze to hold on top of the wound. Then I tried to ball more ripped rags into a dressing. I yelled at Jeff to hold it in place. I could see he was almost losing consciousness. I tried radioing for a medic again. This time I got through, but in the time it took the medic to get to us, Jeff had stopped breathing and no longer had a heartbeat. I was already in the process of CPR and I was trying to bring him back.

While I was doing chest compressions the Doc attempted to seal the wound and check for any unseen injuries. Jeff regained consciousness so we stopped compressions and the doc, now working quickly, focused on the wound telling me to put pressure here and hand him different types of bandages from his bag. I just watched as the Doc started doing chest compressions as Jeff went lifeless again. I could see the emptiness in his eyes as the Doc tried to revive him. Twenty minutes went by and the Doc gave up and called in that Jeff had passed.

I fell to my knees and started balling. I didn't even know Jeff yet I found myself filled with so much emotion of what had just happened I fell apart, crying my eyes out. I looked down and saw Jeff's blood on my hands and my uniform and it just made it worse. I didn't even realize the fire fight had stopped I was so caught up in my own situation. I went back up to finish my post after carrying Jeff down to the HMMV waiting for the Doc and Jeff. The blood was still fresh on the floor as if to haunt and remind me of what had happened. I couldn't stand looking at it so I pulled my poncho out of my pack unfolded it and laid it over the blood stained floor.

I just sat there the rest of my post thinking how I was just standing in front of Jeff. He had just told me to sit and calm down, but I was standing right there in front of him prior to that. We had spotted something, was that the guy that shot him? I ran through multiple scenarios thinking how I obviously failed somehow and I was responsible in some way or another. Chap radioed over to me when he heard what happened. Chap asked if I was ok and tried to get a few answers out of me but I didn't want to talk about it. I just wanted to shoot the bastard who did it.

The Marine that was supposed to be replacing Jeff came on shift. He just sat in the corner not saying anything. He could sense I wasn't in a good mood and just looked out the window of the tower. I don't think he was aware anything happened at all. Nothing ever seemed to be communicated to anyone other than who was involved. Almost like it was on a need to know basis kind of thing. Or maybe no one wanted to know anymore and quit asking. I found myself seeing Jeff's face just lifeless; I tried to block it out. I started wondering if Jeff had a family. Maybe he had a kid or two. What about Jeff's parents did they miss him or would they not care at all. I tried to focus on post and get the thoughts out of my mind but I kept drifting back to what happened and how many more people this had happened to prior to this.

After a while the Marine on post with me started pacing and grabbed his chair to sit down. I just ignored him and looked out the window; it was fairly bright now so seeing anything wasn't a problem. As I was looking out the window I guess he thought I had dropped my poncho and just hadn't gotten around to picking it up so he picked it up. I heard a few muttered profanities as he put it back down. He came over and put his hand on my shoulder and quietly said a soldier's prayer that most of us are familiar with.

"Brave warriors, should fate find us in battle, may our cause be just. May our leaders have clear vision. May our courage not falter. May we be triumphant an earn victory as we show mercy to our enemies. May our efforts bring lasting peace. May our sacrifice be always appreciated by those we serve. May we return to our loved ones unharmed. Should we be harmed, may our wounds heal. Should we perish in the struggle, may God embrace us and find for us a place in his Kingdom."

I found myself with tears in my eyes again. I looked over and he was crying as well. He looked at me with what felt like a familiar feeling as if he'd been where I was now and just said, "Sorry brother, Jeff was a good man." and went back to place his chair and sit down. We both lit a cigarette and stood looking in opposite directions not saying a word. What could you say? What would be appropriate?

He obviously knew Jeff in some capacity but how well? Did he just know him from relieving him or were they close friends like Chap and I, was it appropriate to ask? Nothing came to mind so we just sat there in silence.

The rest of my post went by pretty slow. I was counting the seconds till I was out the door. I wasn't excited anymore, I watched for movement and anything unusual. For the most part I just stayed away from the window and tried not to look at the poncho. I just wanted to get off post and get my stained uniform off me. I wanted to pretend nothing had happened and go back to being excited about being here, but I knew that wasn't going to happen.

I guess I lost track of time and another Marine came up to relieve me. I walked down the stairs and towards the bunk house. I stopped, thought a moment, and decided that wasn't where I wanted to go. Chap would be there waiting to ask me what happened and I still wasn't ready to talk about it so I went to the gym instead. A few Marines stared at me as I went by then I remembered I still had blood stains all over my uniform.

When I got to the gym it was packed full of people trying to work out. I took off my gear and uniform and was down to my skivvies. I felt such relief just getting all of it off. I didn't even work out I just sat there on the bench watching everyone. I guess I didn't realize how tired I was because I dozed off. I woke when Chap punched my chest. I lightly gasped for air and told him in a non-polite manner where to go. He just ignored me and started yelling at me. "What were you thinking not coming back to the bunk? I was worried about you. I heard what happened and have been looking all over for you since we got off post."

I just shrugged and said, "Look man I don't really feel like talking about it. Just let it go." Chap responded. "I'm here for you to talk to when you need it but I'm not going to force you to do anything." Chap and I left it at that and I put my uniform and gear on. Chap gave me an off look. I guess the amount of blood on my uniform startled him. Chap said, "First let's get you a clean uniform. Then you can have some good chow. Then you can get some rest and I promise you'll feel better." Chap and I got to the bunks and I changed into a clean uniform. I didn't feel like eating though I just set the alarm for my next post and went to sleep.

# CHAPTER 3

It was Tuesday—our off duty day, unless we had a mission to go on. But right now, we didn't. I planned on spending most my time collecting scrap metal and aluminum today, if I could find any. I figured I would go around base and get to know who were who and the people worth knowing and avoiding. I put on my gear but left most my ammo. I wouldn't be going out so I only took enough magazines for my M16A2 (Assault Rifle) that I could carry in my pouches. I figured eight should be more than enough. If I went through that I was probably screwed anyways.

My first stop was at the armory, the man of interest there's name was Dan. He controlled who got what ammo and how much. I was looking for armor piercing rounds, not just because I didn't have any, but because when you really wanted to screw something up or stop a vehicle you needed them. That was the real way to do it. Dan was a tall lanky figure; he looked to be well over six feet, which made him look a little awkward because he was so skinny. I had no doubt by the look of him that, lean as he was, he could mess you up pretty quick. Studying his face, I could tell he had his fair share of scuffs. Pair that with the fact that his nose wasn't misshaped or scared let me know Dan didn't lose fights very often at all.

I needed to know what Dan needed before I even attempted asking for what I wanted. I would have to earn his trust and if I was lucky, I could get some scrap metal or he could point me in the direction of some at the same time. I needed the scrap metal first and I knew earning his trust would take a while. I introduced myself and he just gave a shrug as an acknowledgement and kept on working. I decided to see how well he liked being an armorer and play that I needed some supplies to clean my weapons and ammunition.

He almost seemed to get interested, I couldn't tell if he was holding his interest in or was bored and decided to humor me. He went into the back to grab some supplies. While Dan was grabbing the supplies, I looked at the pistol he was working on. It looked like my old 1911 forty-five my father gave me that his grandfather had owned in World War I. As soon as I looked at it, I knew what was wrong: that series had a problem with the safety switch breaking. I swiftly took it completely apart as I had done so many times before, making sure everything was perfectly organized on the table and put the two broken pieces aside. By that time, he had come back and looked flustered that I had taken it apart. Dan was about to yell when I quickly explained to him how I would fix the pin and he didn't have to locate a new one. I would use a torch to get it red hot and bond them back together.

He put the pieces in a Ziploc bag and handed them to me. Dan said, "You fix this for me and I owe you one. Exactly why did you come to me? Someone who knows their way around a weapon like that doesn't need a cleaning kit." I smiled and said, "I'll tell you that when I have the pin fixed for you, for now where can I find scrap metal and aluminum sheets?" He told me about a check point off base that was by a car and salvage scrap yard. Dan said to see a guy named Mahan Mohammed and he could get me whatever I was looking for.

Now I had two things to do, first find someone to fix the damn pin for me or locate a torch to borrow. Second, I needed to volunteer on a patrol going into that area, or find a reason to make my patrol go into that area. There were a few logistics to work out and a lot more people I would need to owe me one before I set out. I was feeling pretty good and it looked like I was one step closer to my goals.

My next stop was to the front gate, at this point I was seeing all the people I would be dealing with over the next few months. Chap at this point caught up to me. "Dude", he said, "What the hell, it's our day off man why are you getting up so early? Plus, what have you been doing the past few hours?" "Relax" I told him, "I've located a scrap yard off base that we need to get to for some supplies." Then showed him the pin, "We need to fix this" I said. He looked at it for a moment, "Let's try the armory." He said. I started laughing really hard and replied, "Well, you got where it came from correct but it's for the armorer. He's busy, it's his, and I said I would fix it." Chap frowned and said, "What are you trying to get from the armory?"

I stopped for a moment before answering, "What happened on the tower got me thinking. They aren't holding any punches and I'm not going to either this is about getting out of here alive with all of you. The way I see it we leave together or not at all."

Chap thought for a moment before replying, "What happened up there?" I know the question was coming but I had all morning to prep for it. I replied, "The guy's name was

Jeff. He died right in front of me and there was nothing I could do about it. What if that was you on post with me? Who's going to take care of your mother if you're gone? She's been sick for years and you keep sending most of your pay to help her pay for all that medicine and doctor visits.

You think your pot-head brother who can't keep a job, or your dead beat Dad is going to change his mind and miraculously come back? I'll be straight up: I don't want to lose my best friend, and your Mom can't afford to lose you either. I promised to watch out for you and that's what I'm doing."

My answer was a little more aggressive than I wanted it to sound but I thought it got my point across. Chap looked at me lightly laughed and said, "Even when you're caring about someone, you're still a selfish bastard and it's all about you. But... you're like a brother to me too and I get what you're trying to say. I trust your intentions at least, but I'm not real sure about your methods though.

Let's go see Jonathan at the repair yard he could probably weld this up fast. Maybe he has a HMMV we could borrow later to check out this scrap yard. We'll have to be tactful about leaving though it's got to be a good excuse."

We started walking to the repair bays and a few mortars started hitting the base. The sirens went off and then a few more landed, one of which hit the barricade in front of us not 10 yards away. We both had dived on the ground, the impact was far enough away not to do much but the dirt and debris had peppered us and the impacts concussion had left our ears ringing. We picked ourselves up and continued on. Chap looked at me and started to speak, "At least they make sure we don't forget we're over here every few hours. Those damn things never stop." I just nodded in agreement and Chap and I kept walking to find Jonathan.

When we got there, he was nose deep in the hood of a HMMV, tossing parts in the sand as he pulled them out. Chap went to the driver side and blew the horn. Jonathan was surprised, slammed up, threw his wrench and said quite a few profanities before calming down. When he finished ranting at us, he looked at Chap and asked, "Why are you here?" Chap replied, "We need a favor."

Chap handed the pin to Jonathan. Jonathan reached in his bag and gave Chap a set of keys and pointed to the gas tanks in the corner of the shop and said, "You boys have fun; you break anything though it's on you." Jonathan went back to work on the HMMV.

Chap passed me the keys and we went to the gas tanks. Chap unlocked the tanks and I adjusted the settings to mix the oxygen and acetylene gas to create a flame capable of melting metal. I used two cinder blocks to hold the pin in place between them and started heating them up. Once they were hot enough, I used the thin rod on the tank holder to fill the broken gaps. I had to make sure it bonded well before I let off. I didn't want to overdo it and ruin the pin either.

I let it cool off and it seemed to do the job. I grabbed the file off the bench and took off all the excess metal from the rod I had used. I left it at that. I figured Dan had whatever equipment necessary to smooth the pin back down at the armory. Chap had been intently watching what I was doing as if to absorb how to do it himself next time. Which I figured might come in handy later if I didn't want to do it myself. I put the tank back the way we got it and locked it back. Then we went back to Jonathan who was still working on the HMMV.

Chap went to hand Jonathan the keys. Jonathan had been waiting for him to come back for a while I guess, because when Chap got to the door Jonathan smacked his hand across Chaps face with God knows what. Chap hit the floor rolling around and gaging. As I watched him suffer it appeared like whatever it was burned and choked him. I looked at Jonathan and asked, "What the hell was that?" Jonathan laughed and replied, "Lemon and onion juice with just a touch of MRE Tobasco sauce. I got hit with it this morning… he's going to be feeling it for a while." Jonathan looked at Chap who was now screaming profanities and punching the sand and said, "If you can't take it, don't dish it." Chap got up and started to laugh as it seemed to be wearing off and said, "I can take it. You win this round and I concede defeat for now."

Chap and I headed back to Dan to give him the pin. When we showed up he seemed a little shocked I was resourceful enough to have it done already. Dan said, "You must know quite a few people to be back so soon. I know you don't have the equipment to fix it. I figured you just might not even come back at all and I'd lost the part and would have to order a new one." I handed him the pin. He looked over before speaking. "It's a little ruff in the center but that's good work and I can smooth it out no problem. So, what's this favor you're going to ask me for now that you've got my attention?"

I looked at him straight faced and stern so he knew I was serious and said, "I need as many armor piercing 5.56mm rounds your willing to give me and a few extra goodies you might happen to throw in with it." Chap looked at me surprised at my request. Dan paused before speaking, "That's a hefty order for someone who just got here." I replied, "That's an order for someone who knows how to get his hands on what people want and need."

Dan went to the back and gave me a small box and said, "This is all the pin bought you. I have a few needs I'd like to get my hands on. You come across any let's say, 'moral and spirit boosters' we will call it, I can give you more." I looked at him and said, "It's a deal." We shook hands and I started heading to the chow hall for some food. It wasn't quite dinner time but I'd missed lunch and breakfast running my errands and wanted to have a full stomach before post. As we sat down to eat Chap seemed a little concerned with what we were acquiring. To ease him off I figured I owed him some answers and explained, "If you're worried about what I'm doing, don't. I'm not planning to use any of it. However, there are a lot of people here who would do quite a bit to get their hands on better ammo and gear to use and have, or even take home. I'm collecting leverage pieces for trade I collect what they want and in return they give me cash or something I want. Let's say for instance a safer time of post for me and my friends?"

Chap perked up at the last part and said, "What do you mean safer time of post?" I responded, "When Jeff got shot, I couldn't see anything, the gate didn't see anything. It was too dark to see anything. The day post has more mortar attacks and more insurgent attacks but at least you can see the bastards coming. If I go, I want to know it was coming. I don't want to go out in the dark like Jeff did."

Chap just patted me on the shoulder and

said, "I feel you buddy, I've got your back don't worry. Your, 'wanting more danger just so you can see it coming' doesn't really make sense to me right now but I'm with you anyway. Chap and I finished up our early dinner. He had two steaks and a potato and I had a few different fruits and a Caesar salad with a bowl of jambalaya. As we got up to leave, I told Chap again to grab a few potatoes. He just laughed and filled his pockets.

He looked at me with a grin and said, "Are you expecting an Irish famine? Starting a potato farm? What's the deal? You haven't even used the other spuds we grabbed." I smiled as I patted my pockets and said, "You'll see when I'm done collecting and you will love me for it." He shrugged and we left to get some rest before our post.

# CHAPTER 4

A week went by and I had been fairly productive in gathering materials, acquiring owed favors and getting to know everyone on base. It was almost as if everyone had been waiting their whole deployment to have someone find things and bring it to them. All it took was leg work, a little charisma, and some sacrifice of your personal time. I don't understand why no one else had ever bothered to do it.

I was in the middle of putting my plan together to go outside the gate to acquire the scrap metal and aluminum sheeting. I knew I needed two HMMV (Basic Hummer, small armored troop transport) to carry everything. Chad and I were in one, but who could I get to go along and drive the other? Dan was too busy. Jonathan was always fixing things or on post, Dave was on opposite shifts. I would either have to change Dave's shifts which would require using a few favors or find someone willing, which I would have to earn trust and an owed favor for that.

Before I even attempted the trip I needed to find out if this Mahan Mohammed had what I wanted. Everyone was shorthanded and over-worked, so no one ever said no to a volunteer who wanted to switch places with them on a patrol, if it meant getting some rest instead. I walked into the briefing room and looked at the map and the patrols that were planned to go out.

I found the perfect patrol; it was going out at midday on Tuesday right by where Mahan was. I wrote down the names on the patrol list and set out to find one of them willing to let me do the patrol in their place. I also had to either bribe or convince the rest to go into, or at least wait at, Mahan's while I spoke to him. Then there was the issue of the translator. I had to make sure I paid him enough to keep him quiet and translate for me, or find something he wanted. It was a short-term loss for long term gain. The whole reason I was going to the scrap yard in the first place was to get the materials to make a boiler so I could make moon shine.

Alcohol is what everyone wanted. There was a little bit of wine circulating. A few smuggled bottles of whiskey. People even had family members mailing it to the in mouth wash bottles. People were paying a lot of money to get their hands on what we called... morale booster or spirit lifter.

The first name on the list I recognized was Youssef. He was a hard charger who enlisted to get his citizenship. He was motto and liked going outside the wire. I noticed his name was on the volunteers list several times for special operations when I was looking at the map, so I didn't think he'd switch. I was almost 100% positive he'd love to have a few emergency armor piercing rounds to stop a suicide car bomber in a spare magazine just in case—as he often went outside the wire.

Chap caught up to me, waiting until I was done talking and handing the rounds to Youssef. I could tell that something was on his mind and he was not looking happy. As soon as I walked away from Youssef and left the room, Chap started talking, "We got pulled off of tower duty both our names are on several of the patrols. Who'd you piss off?" I tried to think of something and nothing in particular came to mind so I just shrugged. Chap started talking again. "You wanted on patrols. You went poking around talking to too many people. Somewhere you either stepped on some ones toes or you found something you weren't supposed to."

If I was in trouble or got caught, no one really had anything on me except the ammo—I must have seen something and didn't realize it when I was looking at the maps. I looked at Chap and started talking, "I must have missed something on the map. Someone thinks I saw something and is trying to say back off. We need to look at the map again but this time without anyone noticing."

Chap shook his head and said, "We don't need any more trouble than what we got. It's bad enough we are just on patrols. That's a borderline death sentence. But to put your hand in a cookie jar that just shut on your hand again?"

I tried remembering all the patrols where they were going and who was going on them. The only one that seemed off was the one we were trying to get on. I looked at Chap and spoke again, "Maybe we don't need to see the map again. I think I might know what's going on. The only real reason to go out as far as Mahan's place would be if you needed something. Someone on the patrol is either smuggling goods on base, or off base. We need to go back inside and talk to Youssef."

"That won't be necessary", Youssef said as he walked toward us. "I'm the guy you're looking for. You're on patrols now and that will keep you out of trouble. Thanks for the ammo by the way, very hard to come by... not sure how you acquired it but it makes me like you. What I don't like is people interrupting what I'm doing. Things work a certain way here: I organize and get things, and people stay happy and no one gets caught or in trouble, do you get it, understand?"

At this point there were two fairly larger Marines behind Chap and I that just showed up, Chap gave me a look of 'I know what you are thinking and that's a bad idea it won't work.' I silently agreed with him knowing we were out maneuvered for now. I said, "I understand." Youssef smiled and said, "Good then we can be friends. You are both on several patrols with me and we are going to have a grand time. You my friend are going to use that skill of yours to help me. As for your friend here, well, suffice it to say he will be with you as long as I am happy." Youssef snapped his fingers and the other Marines left and he went inside.

Chap looked at me in frustration and said, "This is your fault you know. You do all this poking around..." I interrupted him, "Save it.

You already lectured me on my methods. Are you still with me or not?" Chap sighed and rolled his eyes as if I asked a stupid question and said, "I'm always with you aren't I? Let's just make the most of this and get some more of that ammo. I have a feeling we're going to need it."

We headed out to the briefing map to see how many patrols we would be on and how far apart they were from each other. The first patrol was a convoy into the city and some house to house searches. It didn't look like it was going to be that bad: fifteen or so kilometers long, all house-to-house. Intel said low threat in area, but most of the time they were wrong. If they said low threat we could expect medium.

We didn't have long to prep, I ran quickly to see Dan. He was putting away crates of grenades that had been dropped off. Dan saw me and smiled and said, "How can I help my favorite little buddy today?" I responded in a winded fashion, "I need whatever extra power you can give me for a patrol today." Dan looked confused and said, "I thought you were on tower duty tonight?" I replied back, "Well I was but the plan changed." Dan reached in the back and pulled out a shotgun with a shoulder strap full of ammo.

I smiled as I strapped on the rounds and attached the butt of the shot gun to a clip on my shoulder. Dan looked at me with a slight concern and said, "It's none of my business, but getting pulled off tower duty is highly unusual. Either you're in with the wrong crowd or someone's out to get you." I laughed before responding as I started to leave, "Don't worry Dan, I can take care of myself and you are not going to lose any of your gear." Just as I was almost out of the door way Dan's hand was on my shoulder and he put a 9mm with the holster into my back pack with ammo, and a mirror in my front pocket. He nodded to me as I walked out. Dan yelled as I walked away, "Keep it 'til you're off patrols!"

I met Chap at the main gate. There were 3 HMMV's lined up for us to get into. I walked up to Chap and winked at him. He glared at me as if I had slept with his sister or something. I said, "Look I'm sorry you got dragged out here with me. My apology is in my back pack. I need it back after our patrol though." Chap reached in my pack and took out the 9mm ammo and holster. As he put it on I said, "It's yours until we're off patrols." He started to lighten up but still wasn't smiling.

Chap and I got in the middle HMMV, I made Chap sit shotgun while I took the gunner mount. It was a M240 (Medium Machine gun) and she was fairly scarred up. I racked it back to check it out—it was sliding smooth and strong. The ammo bucket was full so I clipped the ammo into top of the M240 and shut the holder. I kicked Chap in the shoulder to let him know I was ready to go.

The drive out there felt good. Having it over 110 degrees constantly outside, a breeze in my face was a nice change of pace. We got to the check point and the drivers backed their vehicles up to one another in a triangle. Once we were all out, the drivers took the gunner mounts of the vehicles and held the position until we all got back.

Youssef came over the head set. "Listen up were doing house-To house in search of a group of known insurgents operating in the area. This is not a light engagement we are undertaking. This is a hot zone; there will be heavy resistance when we find the right house. Do not, I repeat, do not engage on your own when located. Wait for everyone to come to you to assist. We do this together as a team so we can leave together as a team."

Chap looked over to me and said, "What the hell is going on? Who are we getting?" I replied, "Does it matter? They have guns and they are the bad people. We have guns to shoot the bad people." He kicked sand at me to acknowledge my stupid answer to his question. Chap and I were assigned several houses to search and we started heading out, checking windows, roof tops, and doors as we made our way to our targets.

Everyone else split up and went to their objectives. We entered the first house and saw a family eating around the floor. As we scanned the rooms they didn't even move, as if it had happened to them on a daily basis. We cleared each room all the way up to the roof. I used the mirror in my pocket I got from Dan to see if it was clear so I didn't have to stick my head out. Then we went up, Chap went left, I went right and cleared the roof and surrounding buildings roofs.

It seemed fairly quiet for what Youssef called a hot zone. He announced that we found the right house, so we went down stairs and out the back door toward the next house. Over the head set we could hear chatter back and forth about contact front and far right. It was completely on the other side of where Chap and I were but we could hear the gun fire. Youssef came over the head set, "Continue to your objectives—it is a decoy. If you are not engaged in the fight don't join. Find the target house first."

Chap and I were started rush clearing. We knew that everyone in the area knew we were here and probably called in for help. We went through two more houses before we heard an explosion. Whatever it was, it was big, but we had to clear our last target house and go assist whatever was going on. As we came out the back door to go to the last house an insurgent opened up with an AK47 (Assault Rifle).

Chap instantly reacting; put two to the chest and one to the head almost dead on. He rushed to the edge of the door and I laid down cover fire as I was calling in that we were engaging hostiles. I rushed up to kick the door in when several rounds went through the door and into my chest. Before I was even hitting the ground Chap was pulling me to the side and against the wall.

Chap grabbed a grenade and pulled the pin; he held it for almost 3 seconds and threw it in the door. You could hear panicked yells and screams before the grenade went off, then it was silent for a moment. Chap dragged me back to the house we had already cleared to assess the damage. He took the Kevlar plate out of the front and replaced it with the one in my back. Then put the broken one in the back. He smiled at me and said, "Get up salt dog, now that your rear isn't safe you can't retreat."

He helped me up and we went to make a second go at clearing the building. We tossed another grenade in the door for good measure to be sure it went off and we went in. The first room was destroyed, you could see shrapnel marks everywhere from the grenades several dead bodies were on the floor all still clinging lifeless to their weapons. We only paused briefly seeing the damage before moving on.

We cleared the next two rooms without a problem but when we got to the stairwell, we took AK47 fire from the top and neither one of us could get a good angle to go up safely. I rushed up the stairs before Chap could argue who would go first. He quickly followed behind. The insurgent at the top just missed me as I came up into view. I had enough time to lay a good shot into his gut and face. It was the first time I had seen what a spay pattern on a wall looked like and it wouldn't be easily forgotten.

I didn't slow down, I still continued so we could clear the remaining rooms. The next part I wasn't expecting, Youssef came over the head set calling in artillery because the target was found. Chap snatched me real quick and yelled to run. It took a second to sink in then I realized it was our building he had called the strike on. I yelled through the comm unit that we were not clear, but even HQ (Head Quarters) said target was priority and to clear the area—the strike was coming in. We rushed out the back and ran into the street as fast as we could, hoping we would get shot. We had to have a clear distance to get away.

The artillery rounds leveled the building. We had managed to get clear of the blast radius and Chap was yelling profanities about Youssef, HQ and the insurgents. I just let him run off at the mouth and hoped his temper would calm down when we got to the HMMV's. We had about two kilometers to cover to get back to the checkpoint for pickup.

When we got into view of the checkpoint, two of the HMMV's were still smoking from catching on fire. Chap looked at me and said, "Well I guess we found what the explosion was." The other HMMV was in no condition to move and for the moment, we were stranded at the check point with Youssef. Chap looked around and said, "Where is everyone? The drivers are gone and there is no gear, everything has already been field stripped!" I tried the head set but all Chap and I could hear were each other. It was working—just no one was answering.

Youssef and one other Marine with him came into view; we could see they both were carrying what was probably a friend to them.

Youssef started to talk, "I called the order over the head set so you could hear me. I wasn't sure if you made it out. HQ does not care about collateral damage, they want the targets dead. Never forget that while you are out here." As Youssef was talking, I looked him over. He looked like he had taken it worse than we had. His face was stained with dried blood and fresh blood was still running from his nose and right ear.

I could see the head piece from his comm had shattered from whatever did that to his face. The other Marine had a ripped cord, so he wouldn't have been able to communicate either. I looked at Youssef and said, "We would have come to your aide if you would have asked." Youssef looked at me and said, "I wouldn't have asked." Chap remained quiet the whole time I think he was still furious about almost being blasted by our own support.

After sitting for a few hours, a large convoy came to pick us and the ruined HMMV's up. When we got back, the officer in charge of the mission congratulated all of us on a job well done and left. He didn't even stay to show a moment of respect for the Marines that had lost their lives for the mission. Youssef walked up to the two dead, now covered, and said the same prayer I had heard on post. After that he came over to Chap and I and sat down.

Youssef started to talk, "You boys earned your respect here today. We have several more adventures to go one and then you can go back to your dull life." I thought Youssef was going to leave but he was grabbing a crate off the convoy that dropped us off. When he placed it at my feet he smiled and just left. Chap looked at it for a while. As I went to open it he said "Don't!" Inside was more than enough scrap metal and small aluminum sheets for my distillery project. I looked up at Chap and smiled; he uttered a few profanities and then helped me carry the box to our bunk.

# CHAPTER 5

Time went so slow it felt like a prison when you weren't out doing something. We got an emergency call after a few patrols—not sure when it was. A couple of weeks had gone by and nothing big had really happened. You tend to tell how much time has gone by when events happen, other than that it all starts to blur together. I'm not even sure how many patrols we had actually done before today, ten maybe twelve. It felt like one every single day and we were so tired. We can't complain though things have not been that bad up till now.

We had gotten an emergency call; a unit was pinned down by mortar fire and had several groups of insurgents closing in. The insurgents seemed to be pretty coordinated, considering their leader had been killed two weeks ago. Chap and I had found that out a little after the first mission and why HQ was so desperate to be rid of the target.

We set out in HMMV's there were 3 in all. The unit we were going to assist was only 45 minutes out; it wouldn't take long to get to them. They were in a local house made of concrete, giving them ample cover to hold out for a while.

By the time we got there they had 2 wounded and were low on ammo. It looked as if they were at a standoff. The Marine unit pinned down was too injured and low on ammo to attempt an assault. The insurgents however had big enough numbers to cripple the unit.

We started clearing the buildings surrounding them. Chap and I went with another Marine to take the east, while the other two groups headed to the center and west. We started clearing buildings on our way before meeting up with the main unit to insure we had a clear path back to our HMMV's. Chap looked a little concerned and spoke as we were clearing the third building, "I don't feel good about this. There are way too many of them for us not to have run into any one yet. Something's telling me we're about to get crapped on in a very bad way."

I was about to respond to Chap as we went into the fourth building. This was the last building before we got to our destination. That's when they hit us. It was an ambush on the first responders, we were their actual target. An insurgent shot from the roof top then disappeared back inside. Then mortar fire started raining on our position and more insurgents popped up on the roof tops to fire down on us. Chap and I were temporarily pinned down by the back door. I saw a car in my peripheral vision driving to the HMMV's.

I called out on the headset but they were already firing on it. The vehicle didn't stop and exploded at the front of the lead HUMMV. Chap and I were so caught up with the insurgents in front of us that we hadn't noticed a few had gone around the building.

By the time Chap called out on the head set it was too late. Three of them had come in the front door, the first two firing as they came in and took out the other Marine with us. Chap opened fire taking the first two out as I got the third.

We were trying not to get cornered when an RPG (Rocket Propelled Grenade Launcher) flew through the back door. I don't remember hearing or seeing the explosion. All I knew was my ears were ringing and that I needed to pick myself up and continue firing. I did a fast mental body check: my vision was half blurred, I knew I had a pretty bad concussion, and I couldn't tell what else was hurt, but things seemed to move for me. I was at the peak of an adrenalin rush now and had no time to stop and look at what might be wrong. The unit we came to save was now next to us, assisting with covering fire and aiding the wounded and getting them to cover.

They were helping the other two groups that were with us as well, but there were several people missing. Chap helped a Marine carry another Marine that hadn't made it into the secure building we were hiding in. As I scanned the room, I saw six dead Marines. I felt a rage building up inside of me. Stupid or not, I was going to do something about it. I don't even know if Chap saw me dash out.

I shouted for cover as I headed into the first building that had multiple insurgents on the roof. I cleared the whole building with no resistance until I came to the top. They hadn't seen me go in the building; I figured I had the jump on them, there were six in total. I called for a distraction. I wasn't expecting them to launch a grenade up, but it did the trick. They tried to scatter but it went off, killing three of them, leaving the other three in shock. I rushed through the door, subduing them with ease and zip tied their hands and feet. They were in no condition to fight back after the explosion. I turned to snipe the rest of the insurgents on the roof tops.

The fire fight was under control, minus the

mortars still landing. I realized how hurt I was when I tried to go down the stairs and collapsed. I rolled to the bottom and arm crawled to the door. Chap saw me and ran to assist, dragging me to safety. I told him to retrieve the prisoners; he nodded as I started to pass out from blood loss.

When I came to I was in a make shift infirmary. I could tell it had been mortared more than a few times since it had been put up. I remembered what happed and quickly checked fingers, toes, and limbs. A few bandages were here and there, and I felt sore all over. I noted that it was nothing too bad, based on how I felt. It was like I got in a car crash and didn't wear my seat belt, yet miraculously didn't break anything. My head was still pounding and I felt nauseous as I tried to get up. I had to know how everyone else was.

I didn't get far before a captain stopped me and told me to sit. I waited until he wasn't looking and ducked out the front. I quickly realized I had no clue where I or where the rest of my unit was. I bummed a smoke from the Korean soldier by the butt can and puffed slow and deep. I held my breath to take in the nicotine for a calming buzz. I didn't want to be out here but I needed to talk to Chap. I hoped he was okay. I figured he was probably mad at me as always. As I finished my smoke the captain came out side and told me to come inside. I guess he had been looking for me.

He said he needed to do one last check up on me and I was free to go home. I looked at him in a very serious manner and said, "Respectfully Sir, I'm going back to my unit, if they aren't going home I'm not either." He smiled and said I wasn't the first to say that. He gave me a form to sign so I could return back to my unit.

It took two days to get back and I still hadn't figured out how long I had been gone. I figured Chap would fill me in when I got back to the bunk but he was asleep when I came in. I left him alone—I wasn't sure if he had post, or a patrol or anything and didn't want to ruin whatever routine he made while I was away.

I looked at my bunk and couldn't help but laugh. While I was gone, someone took all my aluminum sheets and scrap metal and built the boiler. Now we could make some moonshine with potatoes and yeast. Chap must have talked to Jonathan—he's the only one I know that can weld that good.

It felt good to get in my bunk and I take a rest. Not too long after that, Chap woke me up like I figured he would. He horsed me and said, "Why didn't you tell me you were back? We were all worried about you." He waited for me to climb out of the bunk "Are you ok?" he asked. When I nodded my head that I was he clocked me a good one. He had hit me so hard I lost my balance and hit the floor. I didn't even see it coming and I couldn't react to it.

He stood above me and asked, "Well?"

I guess he was expecting a fight after he hit me but after the way I took off without him in the firefight I couldn't get upset with him. I didn't want him to go with me, just in case. Running in was pretty damn stupid and I didn't want Chap killed because of my stupidity. I started lightly laughing as I got up and said, "I love you too brother."

Chap frowned and said, "If you pull a stunt like that again without taking me with you, I will shoot you myself." I half-laughed again and gave Chap a pat in the back. I could feel my jaw now really starting to hurt. I looked at my boiler and asked, "So, you seem to be resourceful enough without me?" Chap smiled and said, "I'm a fast learner. I had seen your plans on the bunk before, so I knew what your plan was the whole time. I figured it would make a nice welcome back gift."

Chap had a concerned look on his face as he spoke, "I thought for sure you might just take the easy way out and go home." I started setting up the boiler as I spoke, "I couldn't leave you out here without me. You'd have no one to keep out of trouble, and you would die of boredom." Chap helped me finish setting up the boiler. She didn't look pretty but I knew it would do the job.

We filled it with water, peeled all the potatoes and then put them in as well. The make shift distillery had to do its job now. The potatoes had to boil down to mush before the next stage. We used the propane lamps we had as the heat source and let her run. It would take a while to have the finished product but it was worth the wait. Chap looked at me now that we were finished and spoke. "You promised to fill me in when it was done, so fill me in."

I drew a make shift map in the dirt and started explaining, "Most of the batches will be for our small circle. The extra that we have is going to be used for trading and cash." I pointed at the dirt map as I spoke again, "These bunks here have people gambling and buying whiskey and wine, these here are the officers that have been buying a lot of the smuggled goods to send home and have been asking around for better goods. Finally, these here are the safe drink areas where everyone who's been buying is drinking."

I sat on the bunk before continuing, "I've done a tally since we've been here, and everyone has bought something at some point in time—including the brass. The key thing to remember is the higher up they are the better quality product they expect." Chap looked at the map and smoothed it out with the bottom of his boot before speaking. "We make the batches, we drink the batches. Put the other bottles away for a rainy day. Let's not make our stay here any more difficult than it already is."

I thought for a moment and decided I agreed with Chap and spoke, "Ok, I'm with you on this one. I owe you too much not to listen to your opinion and advice. By the way thanks for everything, and I don't mean the boiler, for saving my ass." Chap nodded and looked at the broiler working and smiled before he spoke, "So how long does this process take?"

I laughed before speaking, "Well, first the potatoes have to boil to mush for a while. After that we let it cool down to room temperature and put the yeast in. It has to sit one to three days depending on how long it keeps foaming. Then we distill it in the tube portion of the boiler three times. The first batch we might have to throw away. Sometimes it turns bad for the boilers first use, so don't plan on drinking this one, but for sure the next."

Chap smiled and signaled me with his hand to follow him so I did. He took me to the briefing room to the map. As I looked it over a few hot spots had changed and new patrols were posted for going out. Chap looked up as he spoke, "You were gone four days but a few things have changed, I have my own patrols now and I want you on them." He pointed to the patrols on the upper portion of the map where the fighting was thickest.

I looked and asked, "What did I miss?" Chap smiled and answered, "Between being with you and the shit that hit the fan when you left, I got a combat promotion and new job duties. They wanted someone level headed to deal with the worst areas."

I looked at him and spoke, "I thought you wanted safe?" Chap replied, "After I saw those Marines we came in to save, they ended up saving us instead. I realized no one really knows what they are doing. They are all as new to this as we are. If anyone is going to put us in harm's way it should be us. Not like you never put us in harm's way to begin with." I started laughing as I spoke, "Yeah I tend to do that don't I? Fair enough, it's your turn to get us shot at. I'm with you buddy."

Chap smiled and lightly punched my arm as thanks for the support. We headed to the chow hall to get some food. He had us on a listed patrol almost every day. I did notice he kept Sundays off the patrol list, but I would ask him about our plan for off time later.

When we got to the chow hall I could smell the seafood from outside. My senses didn't want to believe what I smelled.

Sure enough, we walked in and they had lobster tails and crab legs on the buffet. According to the sign they had up, it was going to be a biweekly thing too. Talk about the royal treatment! That was a luxury I thought I would never see again. Chap and I piled our plates up. Over an hour passed and we were stuffed, I lost count of how much we ate. By the looks of everyone around us they were all doing the same. Chap and I washed up to get the seafood smell off and headed back to the bunk.

When we got to the bunk and checked the boiler it had done an excellent job on the potatoes. We turned it off to let it cool down and would have to wait for it to reach room temperature before adding the yeast to it. Chap looked at me and asked. "What gave you this idea anyways?" I laughed and replied, "My older family used to talk about the prohibition a lot where I come from. The one that stuck most was how this Sheriff kept trying to find a moonshiners stash in the swamp. According to the story, an old man had the best moonshine around. One small cup was enough to knock you out."

Chap interrupted, "Did the Sheriff ever get him?" I smiled and continued, "The Sheriff couldn't find the boiler because the farmer hid it by an alligator's nest. But that's not the point of my story. The reason I liked it was no one liked the taste, but everyone wanted the kick. That's what everyone here is looking for, including me. We drink to relax or we drink to forget, but either way: we drink." "Not everyone drinks." Chap responded. I laughed and quickly replied, "The ones still alive do. The dead ones don't have a choice."

Chap gave me a look but then started setting up his gear and cleaning the 9mm pistol I gave him. Chap looked up at me and smirked. I asked, "What did I miss?" He laughed and responded, "You know I'm your squad leader now right?" I laughed and pushed him over. He started laughing and continued cleaning the pistol.

# CHAPTER 6

Dave came by to talk to me while I was cleaning my weapons. I tried to maintain them consistently. The sand was so bad here and got into everything, even if you had it sealed. As he walked into the room, I happily greeted him and asked him to have a seat. I could tell by the way he walked in he wanted me to ask him what was going on. It obviously wasn't just a social visit on a day that he was supposed to be on shift. I spoke up, "What can I do for you Dave? I can tell you've got something on your mind." He hesitated before speaking, "Chap and you are the talk of everyone lately, and everyone seems to be jealous, even me. I still don't have my combat action ribbon yet…" He paused as to leave it open for me.

I started speaking again, "So you want to come with us you mean, just one patrol—

maybe two? All of them?" Dave looked down as if embarrassed for even asking. He started speaking, "I don't exactly know what I want… I guess just the ribbon and the chance to see if I can do what you guys do."

I laughed and asked, "What do you mean 'do what you guys do.'?" He spoke with more confidence, "I want to know if I'm the guy that drops and hides, or if I've got what it takes to face the fire and do what needs to be done." I started replied, "Look, if you want the ribbon, I can do that for you. If you want the experience—this isn't a game you can come out of where either you make it or you don't. You're a good friend and I'm not going to sugar coat it for you. We carry full gear and are out some times for several days, there's little sleep in-between and we usually don't come back in until we either find what we are looking for or run into trouble the insurgents set up for us. It sucks, people die, and you can't undo any of it." Dave looked as if I insulted him and started talking, "I need to know what kind of Marine I've turned out to be. I went through everything you did to get here and I'm stuck here and you are out there. I should be out there with you and Chap."

There were a few minutes of silence between the two of us. "Ok." I said. Dave looked up surprised and spoke with enthusiasm, "I can go?" I replied, "Let me work out the logistics with Chap, but yes, I will try to get you on our patrols." Dave jumped up with excitement and said, "Wait till I tell Jonathan—he's not going to believe I'm going!" He bolted out of the room to tell Jonathan, half giddy and laughing as he went out. I continued cleaning my weapons and was now working through my head how to convince Chap to add Dave to our patrol list.

Almost an hour had gone by before Chap walked into the room. I had already worked out my plan and began executing it. I set a can of beer down in front of him that I had bought off of a British soldier I had been hanging out with lately. We met on a patrol a few days earlier and I pulled him out of a tight spot. He kept randomly running into me and we would sit and talk about the differences in our countries for a while and then part ways. Chap picked up the beer and looked at me with a stern scold and spoke, "What did you do or break?" I laughed and responded, "Open it, have a drink, sit down and hear me out." Chap opened the beer smelled it then smiled and spoke, "I don't know why or how you keep getting such great gifts to give, but I thank God that you do every time you share them with me." He took a long sip with a look of ecstasy on his face and then passed the can to me for a drink.

I took a sip then passed it back and began talking, "Dave came by today to talk to me, he would like to come on a few patrols. Maybe even stay on for the rest of the deployment." Chap pulled out a sheet of paper he had in his back pocket. He began speaking, "I want you to take a good, hard look at this list." I grabbed the list; I knew he was going to do something along the lines of it as soon as I saw what it was. It was a list of names, of Marines, soldiers, and internationals that had lost their lives on the patrols we had been going on. It didn't seem like a big list at first, but when you think of how long we had been there it hit a little home to the danger we kept facing. I looked up and spoke, "Look, he came to me because he wanted to go. If he wanted to be talked out of it, he would have come to you instead. He knows the danger and what's on the line. Let him make the choice. At least talk to him and give him the chance to decide for himself. No one wants regrets when you leave this place—we already have enough of those."

Chap finished the beer on his own before getting up and looked at me in the eyes as he spoke, "I'll talk to him, if only to talk some sense into him. If that doesn't work, then one patrol is all he gets. One. No more. Secondly: don't start making promises you can't keep. This is your one favor that isn't reusable if he decides to go."

Chap slammed the door as he walked out. I knew he was going to pull the mother hen routine on it, but if Dave wanted to go, he should go. I thought about going after Chap but then decided the possible fight we would get into wasn't worth trying to push my point any further. He thought I was wrong for even asking for Dave, and that wouldn't change.

I didn't see Chap for quite a while after that—he must have still been mad at me. He should have caught up with Dave fairly fast. I decided to go for a walk; I needed to refill my flask of moon shine for the poker game tonight anyways. I had a nice spot that was out of site and I hid the jugs once they were made. You didn't want to get caught if anyone searched your bunk house. Took a while to find a good location no one would go into. I had it under a plate in the roof of the building next door. The plate weight almost 40 lbs. so no one would bother picking it up most people were too lazy in this heat. The down side was the moon shine was always more than luke-warm when we picked it up.

After filling my flask I took a quick swig and headed on my walk to think and wander around a bit. I had been fairly busy lately and I hadn't had time to trade or deal with Youssef. I figured I would drop in on the local smuggler to see how he was doing and if there was anything new he had scrounged up worth trading for or at least, getting myself. After a long walk I found him by the armory dealing with Dan. From a distance it looked like a trade of some sort but Youssef was fairly good at concealing what he was doing. I gave a shout to him so he would know I was looking for him and not snooping.

Youssef quickly concluded his business with Dan as I was walked up. He started walking towards me; arms open as he spoke, "My friend you have come to grace me with your presence. I haven't seen you in too long. Your visit is overdue as is your payment for your last purchase." He grimly smiled as he finished the last sentence. I smirked as I spoke, "Your payment is in route, some things are harder to acquire than others as you well know."

Youssef gestured for me to walk with him. He began speaking as I followed, "It is good that you have come to see me. I have another item of which I would like to acquire."

"First, what is this item you wish to acquire and second, where do you think it might be located that you can't get it yourself?" I asked. Youssef replied, "You have a patrol listed on the map, a week from now, going through a rough section that is a hot zone and has not been cleared. It is fairly dangerous and you'd have to have a better reason than I can come up with to just walk around there. You luckily are already scheduled for a heavy escort and extraction of a local informant there, so you don't need an excuse." He pulled out a copy of the map and started talking again, "Your escort and extraction goes through this small town where I lost a valuable shipment for an extremely important person on this base. You don't open the package. It is located on the roof of the building on the furthest edge of the town. You bring it to me, no questions asked. That is what I need you to do for me."

I stared at the map for a moment and spoke, "That's quite the detour from the planned path... I should be able to acquire it for you. I'll have an answer this afternoon. As for payment: I have a friend who owes your poker dealer quite a bit." Youssef smiled before speaking, "This is no small favor I ask of you and worth more than your friend owes. Think on it hard because, if you fail after accepting, I'm not the one who will be talking to you. The owner of the package will and you don't want to meet with him. It can be hazardous to your health and mine." I looked the map over once more and spoke, "This must be quite the package. How did you lose it in the first place?" Youssef looked a little sad as he spoke, "A good friend of mine ran into some complications and had to leave it on the roof, sadly he did not make it back, nor did the package."

"He was, however, able to tell us where he hid the package as he was taking cover so we could extract them both. We were too late and the extraction team was not equipped for house-to-house with what they encountered. They lost a few good men before they pulled back to base empty handed. You and Chap have the best equipment and team around. If you do this for me, then whatever you ask that I can get or give is yours. Think on that as you go and figure out what you need to do." I didn't respond. I just turned and walked away. I would have to convince Chap, he was racking up quite the debt gambling. Maybe wiping his sheet clean would be enough to convince him that it was worth it.

As I headed back to the bunks I didn't get too far before Chap was hailing me. As he walked up, I spoke, "Just the man I was coming to see." He didn't smile and spoke, "I was about to say the same to you but I'm not as enthusiastic as you about it. Dave will be on patrol with us for a few weeks to get his feet wet, nothing more nothing less. Our light scheduled patrols only, until he proves himself otherwise." I smiled before talking, "Good I wasn't expecting anything else. I'm going to be blunt here, what's your debt up to at the local poker game, eight grand now?" Chap turned a little red as if embarrassed and spoke, I played again without you last night. I thought I could win it back... I had to sign another note." I frowned now agitated and spoke." You know not to play without me and this is why. How much is it this time?"

Chap looked at the ground kicking sand as he spoke, "Another five thousand." I about choked before I spoke, "Holy crap Chap, you are never going to pay that back! I think I have got it figured out though, there's a package for Youssef on one of our runs. We get it and we can wipe your debt clean." Chap looked at me a little worriedly as he asked, "Exactly what is this we are picking up that could clean out that much debt? Don't get me wrong I want it gone but it must be something very illegal or extremely dangerous." I replied, "It is probably both, and part of the conditions is to not know what is in the package, and to not open the package." Chap spoke again, "Exactly where is this so called package we are picking up?" I replied, "Right on the way back from extracting the informant we dropped off last week."

Chap frowned as he spoke, "You mean the hot zone portion of that trip don't you?" I smirked and spoke, "Relax. We have a full team. They can continue on route to deliver the informant. You and I with a spare HMMV can go get the package from the roof of the building in the far corner." Chap thought about it for a moment before speaking again, "This will clear my debt you say?" I nodded my head, "Straight from Youssef. Your debt was below what the package is worth to him." Chap thought for a moment before continuing, "Alright. We'll do it." I nodded and we continued to the bunk house. He reached into my pouch where he knew my flask was to take a swig and said, "Let's pick up a little extra for tonight." I laughed and we kept walking.

We got back to the bunk and started drinking pretty heavily; it had been a rough week. Between Chaps gambling getting worse and regular patrols to the hot zone to make it safer—it was starting to take a toll on us. Chap had started to have night terrors and hallucinations. I didn't tell him I knew yet, but I figured he probably knew I did. He had started drinking more and gambling a lot to blow off steam—but the gambling got bad and now he started stressing over how much he owed. I played to help lower his debt for him and had been doing a few favors here and there to drop it. He had gotten so bad with it I don't think he even noticed. I just sat there and continued to sip my flask enjoying the warmth and burn as it ran down my throat. Thinking to myself 'We are not going to have a choice if we are going to fix this problem.'

I looked over to Chap as I started to feel the alcohol work its magic; he was already passed out on the floor. I walked over to him and lifted him to his rack and made sure he was breathing. Content that he looked comfortable enough and I could feel his breath on the back of my hand, I stumbled to my chair to sit down. Then the alcohol started hitting me pretty hard. I laughed to myself as I considered where we were in our lives. Here we are; the best of our group doing the most dangerous job there was. On the outside, people were in awe of what we do. We are the heroes, saviors, and great leaders. Just as soon as we go behind closed doors the pressure shows—we are habit ridden and broken beyond repair. Our minds damaged goods that do nothing but play tricks on us. As I strained to try and think straight the darkness took me and I passed out.

I woke up to Chap kicking me in the side as he spoke, "Wake up time to go for a quick run then we will go get some chow." I said a few profanities as I rolled over and flipped him the bird. Chap helped me up and I went to my gear for our running set. We were in boots, pants, tee shirt and flak jacket with full ammo loads for our run. It helped to keep us conditioned for combat conditions and our bodies in the habit of always being under a load and pushed. Today's goal was several laps around the base to sweat off the booze. We would know when we were good when both of us puked from being pushed too far.

We could usually go longer after that but neither one of us liked to. We did it enough times that the limit always got further and further anyways. We started to walk to our usual point by the wall of the base and stretched before we would take off. Chap looked at me. I nodded that I was ready and we went. 'It's a hot day' I was thinking as I could feel the burn on my skin as we were running. Chap had a nice pace going, my legs were a tad shorter so I couldn't stride as well as he did, but it did me good to keep up with him. By myself I tended to get lazy and I didn't push hard enough, but with Chap it's almost a goal to see who can go the furthest without puking first. I could tell he was feeling the drinking from last night he seemed to be lagging a bit, I always could drink him under the table. It didn't deter him from trying to outdo me anyway; he always took joy in beating me at anything he could. We finished our first round it was about a full kilometer around the base. We weren't sure exactly because the route we ran would change every time due to vehicles or quad cons being in the way and blocking older paths. We continued through the second lap and I was feeling it. At this point my lungs are a little on fire from the dry air and my chest is starting to feel that pain right before you get a second wind, I just had to keep up and push past the pain.

Third lap, pain in my chest is starting to settle. My second wind is hitting as well as the adrenalin rush from pushing my body in the heat. You get an endorphin effect from it or a high that makes you feel great for a moment as you're pushing past it. Almost on lap four. I can feel my legs starting to go soft and have to keep telling myself 'left, then right' and repeating it over and over so as not to trip as my mind starts to give way from dehydration during the run. I had to keep going, but I couldn't hold the pace any more.

I started to drop back; I could hear Chap start to laugh as he said, "Just let it out." Chap kept running around me to keep his pace going as I started to throw up in the sand.

I got up and started to run again. Now I had the lead and with the small break, should be good to push Chap past his edge. We learned to throw in a few exercise drills after I lost. I randomly stopped and yelled, "Push!" Chap dropped and did twenty pushups, before he could get on his feet I yelled, "Climb!" Chap quickly went to mountain climbers twenty reps again, then to my favorite part as he got up I yelled, "Sprint!" We both made a mad dash as fast as we could. Not even fifteen seconds into the sprint Chap started throwing up. I guess it wasn't exactly fair but it wasn't supposed to be fair. The whole point was push till you break.

Once we were done running, we headed to the bunk and put all our gear away. Chap and I quickly got dressed to go to chow and headed out. Breakfast was eggs and several options of meat and vegetables to go with it.

I had two omelets with tomatoes ham and mushrooms. Chap had two with ham, bell peppers and hot sauce. I always loved eating after we would run. The food always seemed to taste better. Most likely it was because we were starving after making ourselves sick for the run. I let my mind wander off as we ate. It was the most relaxed I had been in a while and I wanted to savor that feeling while it lasted. It didn't happen very often any more.

With the upcoming patrols, that relaxed feeling was needed more than ever. It was going to be a rough week or so. Chap had several dangerous runs planned through the hot zone. There were a few light patrols in-between to give us a break but, for the most part, we would be going at it pretty fast and hard. Chap seemed a little more relaxed than usual. It made me wonder and I wasn't sure if it was for the same reason I was. Was it just a good feeling from the run or was it the thought of paying off his debt? Either way it was good to see him relaxed. It made me feel more at ease in the moment.

# CHAPTER 7

The past week was pretty uneventful which was great. Dave seemed happy he was on patrols with us. It appeared as if everything was working out like I wanted it to for now. I started a poker group of my own to keep Chap occupied and satisfy his need to play. Buy in was only twenty dollars versus the five hundred dollar table he kept going to. I had been spotting him money until we could get the situation handled. I felt bad for Chap, normally I was the one with the problem and he watched out for me. Now he had the problem and I was watching out for him. I couldn't quite understand his urge to bet everything on a chance to win. All he would keep saying is 'I can win it back' but he never would.

I think a lot now instead of talking. Right now, I'm pondering about Chap's gambling need. I guess it's no different than my need to plant bad ideas in his mind. I'm always doing something to keep my mind occupied. It just always leads to trouble and he has to bail me out or help me. The benefits seem to outweigh the consequences in my mind. He probably sees it the same way with his gambling. When you're hooked on an activity everything around you just zones out and you live in the moment. It's like nothing else exists.

That is until reality hits you when it's over and then you have to pick up the pieces. If I look at it that way, I can see how he can get lost in the moment. Could I have driven him to the habit? Most likely it was this place—who knows for sure what makes us do the things we do?

As I was sitting in my bunk, Jonathan walked in carrying a box and said, "Your long awaited package has arrived from the states." He dropped the box on the foot of the bed and sat in my chair. I gave him a fake salute and started opening the box. I pulled out a canister and sleeve, along with some fireworks at the bottom of the box. I wanted to inspect them prior to giving them to Youssef. When he gave me my materials for the boiler, he neglected to tell me that I owed him. His payment would be fireworks and I figured they were easy enough to smuggle in. We sent in shipments of arms and vehicle parts all the time to get repaired and sent back. It pays to know a lot of people that owe you a favor or two.

I put everything in my pack and shook Jonathan's hand saying, "Thanks bud. I'll meet you after I deliver them to Youssef." Jonathan didn't say anything. He just lightly slugged my shoulder and left. I walked out behind him, but not in the same direction. I wanted to deliver the package and get off his debt list. Owing people is bad for acquiring things—it is supposed to be the other way around. I should hang out with Jonathan after I'm done with Youssef. I haven't had a good talk with him in over a month now.

Everything is so hectic and our schedules rarely seem to work together.

I got to Youssef's place. I could hear arguing and what sounded like a fight after. I didn't want to barge into something I would regret, so I stood to the side and listened. I could hear a deep voice say, "Don't disappoint me again." Then it sounded like someone got punched and hit the floor hard. I saw two thick Marines walking out first. They looked around and gestured to an older Marine. They quickly got into the HMMV in front of the building and left. When I was sure it was clear I walked in to see if it was Youssef they had roughed up.

I was surprised to see Youssef only had a scratch on his face. I spoke as I walked in, "That sounded a lot worse from outside." Youssef took off his shirt to assess the damage himself. That's when I could see the bruising and welts. "Never mind" I said. Youssef looked at me and spoke, "I need that package soon. He's getting impatient."

I spoke, "I don't know what you did to owe him that package, but you might not want to owe that guy anything. It's bad for business and bad for your health. You lose favors and good people to guys like that. Force is never necessary to acquire anything. Just time, patience and a little leg work." Youssef looked up and spoke, "Guys like that find you and demand things. There is no favor or owing.

You've hid well so far and only because he thinks I operate the whole base. Once he finds you, there is no getting away." I looked around the room and at all the things Youssef had acquired in his time here. "Your problem is, it's obvious to someone like me what you spend your time doing." I said, "If I can tell, so can anyone else who wants to know. As for me, well you'll have a hard time convincing anyone that a guy with an empty bunk has anything." Youssef stared at me for a moment before speaking, "He will find out sooner or later. I was here for my second tour when he found me. How long will your network here survive when you go back home? Who do you think will take it over and get information on you when you leave?" I smiled as I spoke, "My network? That's a laugh, which just proves my point even more. You don't even know how I operate and I deal with you quite a bit. It's about stealth and technique. You create trust and bonds that only work for you and no one else. There is nothing to take over when I leave."

Youssef frowned as he spoke, "No one operates like that forever. Your people will die one by one, maybe not today, but eventually. You will still need things and will have to find someone else. I used to work like you once. You learn here that you can't rely on people being alive too long. You need a better plan than that." I just shook my head as I spoke, "I acquire things to help people that I care for. The profit is just a side effect. If there are no people to care for, then there is nothing worth acquiring." After that I just left. I was a little mad, but he got himself into that mess and I wasn't going to dig him out. My only concern was clearing Chap's debt to

Youssef's dealer.

We had a patrol coming up and I didn't have time to waste. I wanted to at least see Jonathan before I left on patrol again, I really hated it that our paths rarely crossed anymore. I headed to the vehicle repair yard where he was usually working or hanging out. I don't think he ever left that place unless he was coming to see Chap and I. Sure enough, as I walked into the yard he was as usual inside the hood of the HMMV sitting on the edge with his feet on the motor. He was clean when I saw him earlier. But now he was covered in grease and dirt. He must have been underneath at some point because there was sand on the grease stains on his back.

I gave Jonathan a wave when he saw me. He just nodded and went back to working under the hood. I could hear a few profanities as I came up behind him. It looked like he banged his knuckle trying to remove something. I lightly laughed and had to duck quickly as the wrench he was using came at me. "You missed." I said as I picked up the wrench. He laughed and replied, "If I wanted to actually hit you I would have aimed." I handed the wrench back to him and started said, "You've been busy. I haven't seen you in a while. Are you doing alright?" Jonathan kind of shrugged as he replied, "Yeah, I guess. I've been so busy with repairs I hadn't really had time for much else."

There was a long pause before Jonathan started talking again, "I've been meaning to see the doc about my hearing loss. Took a few IED impacts while doing a few convoy runs with the EOD (Explosive Ordinance Disposal) team. They just said to suck it up. Everyone is going through it. They thought I was trying to push for a combat action ribbon. I just wanted to get rid of my headaches and get some Motrin and eardrops or something." I thought before I started to speak, "If you want to see the Doc, go see the Doc. Get what you need. Don't worry about the paper work and they won't harass you about anything. You've got to take care of yourself because no one outside of us is going to. Everyone here only cares about their job and how much work they have to do. No one cares how sore, beat, tired, depressed, and injured you are. None of that matters to anyone except us. So if you need it, go get it."

There was a long pause again. Jonathan looked up as he spoke, "I just want to do my job and go home. I'm tired of this place. I never wanted to be here to begin with." I smiled and put my hand on his shoulder and said, "I know buddy. That's why we came along. Why don't you go see Chap and play in tonight's poker game with him? He'd like that. Dave's on patrol with us tonight. I'll make him go too." Jonathan seemed to cheer up a bit as he spoke, "Is there going to be any moral boosting there?" I laughed and responded, "I'll have a separate one ready just for you." Jonathan now looking excited went back to work on the motor. I headed back to my bunk.

Chap was there waiting on me, right by my bunk. I opened my gear box and started getting ready for our patrol. Chap looked at me and laughed as he started talking, "Cutting it pretty close aren't you?" I responded, "Nah, I knew I had enough time. After patrol we've got a poker game with Dave and Jonathan." Chap seemed to lighten up, "Really? That's great. All of us haven't been together since we got to this hell hole." He said. "I know," I said. I continued packing. It didn't take me long. I kept everything in order and ready. Chap stood up and grabbed his pack. He was already in full gear.

I still had to put mine on; I grabbed my flak jacket, made sure the plates in the front and back were straight, buttoned it up, and closed the Velcro seam. It takes a while to get used to the neck guard but as I put it on almost a comfort feeling crosses you as it wraps your neck in appearing safety, I almost feel naked without it now. I fill my pouches with ammo and snacks; put candy in my cargo pocket for throwing to the kids. I check my rifle and shot gun—they're good. I put the shot gun on my shoulder clip, then my pack on my back. My camel pack is full of water. I was ready.

Chap and I headed to the pad where our patrol HMMV's were. There were eight in all for today's patrol. We were doing a foot and mount patrol. It was a combination of using the HMMV's to run down targets as the people on foot flushed them out of buildings. It usually ended in a rough fire fight but nothing too major. It was a simple medium patrol with no problems expected. Dave was already in our HMMV. Chap had made him our driver for this patrol. Dave didn't quite have the physical capability to go on foot for very long in full gear. He did however prove that he had some excellent driving reflexes when it came to IED's in the road.

It was almost as if Dave had a sixth sense about where they were located. We hadn't hit one since Dave started driving. This was unfortunate for those behind us, because that usually meant one of them hit what we missed. Dave gave a thumbs-up for us to see that everything in our HMMV was ready to go. Chap walked down the line, checking everyone's gear and asking questions about things being ready. He checked everyone's water levels and fuel, careful not to miss anything. His checks always seemed to last at least thirty minutes. He wanted to make sure we were prepared as well as possible. Once Chap was content that we had what we needed and everyone was ready, he blew his bull horn and got in the HMMV. I quickly climbed into the gunner's seat and checked that it racked right. The M249 SAW looked good. I put the ammo in and closed the top.

We rolled out the gate and I racked it back with the ammo to be ready to fire at a moment's notice. We drove by a farmer's field and could hear one of the other guys in the convoy commenting on the farmer in the field beating his wife with a stick. We all watched as we drove by. As horrible as it was, we were not allowed to get involved in those affairs. Even going over there to stop him would cause a big political problem that would ruin your career. So, we watched as we passed. Painfully it was all we could do.

There was less and less green in the scenery as we got further away from the river, and soon there would be no green at all. We closed in on the village we were going to search. The patrol pulled over to let out all the Marines going on foot. We were going in teams of four on foot and teams of two in the HMMV's. Chap and I were going with two other Marines in the last vehicle. The Marine in the back passenger seat of our HMMV was gunning while Dave was driving.

I was on point with Chap who was leading not only our team, but the whole operation. Chap gave the signal and the HMMV's started to do a complete circle around the small village, putting enough distance between each other that they could cover anyone trying to leave. Chap gave the next signal and we all moved in. We all knew our routes and which houses to search. The only question now was: who was going to get the targets?

I entered the first house, Chap close behind me along with the other two Marines. We kept close quarters like this for our whole search. Nothing in the first house so we headed to the second, as we entered the second, I could hear in my head piece, contact front house number seven. Chap motioned us to hold and pulled out his map. Chap then called a few commands over the head set to the HMMV to change formation and one went to the building to assist. Chap then motioned for us to continue.

As we cleared the second house, we could hear echoes of random fire. It was hard to tell where they were coming from. Every so often we kept stopping and Chap would check the map and give a few more movement changes and we would continue. As we were going through the houses, no matter how many times I saw it, I was amazed. The locals never reacted. They just kept going about their business as if nothing was happening;

only ducking when they could hear shots. Even the kids playing with their wooden or handmade toys acted as if nothing was going on.

We were almost at the end of the search. It was crunch time. We forced the hiding insurgents into a corner of the village which was the goal. There hadn't been any shots for a few minutes. Then, a few insurgents came out with their hands in the air waving that they were surrendering. We converged on their spot yelling at them to lift their shirts so we could see if they had any hidden weapons or if one was a suicide bomber. They were unarmed. They all lay on the ground as the other teams zip tied their hands behind their backs and put hoods over their heads so they couldn't see where they were going.

Chap signaled for everyone to return to the HMMV's with the detainees and head back to base. When we arrived, we took them to the detention cell where a few guards were stationed to watch that they didn't escape.

There were two already in the hold. It wasn't much of a cell. It was made of chicken wire and razor wire—maybe about twelve feet wide in both directions and six feet high. The detainees were all placed in there facing away from each other and an interpreter was left close by to listen to any conversations they might have.

As I pulled my gear to the HMMV I yelled to Dave, "When you park it come to my bunk." Dave smiled and gave a thumb up as if he already knew what was going to happen there. Dave drove off and I started heading back to the bunk. Chap was debriefing and doing whatever paper work he had to do for rounds fired and the two injuries we had taken. One injury was a new Marine on patrol with us who had taken a round to the shoulder. The other was one of the interpreters with us. He had taken a round to the leg.

Jonathan was already at the bunk waiting; I passed him four flasks and told him where the stash was. He excitedly left almost skipping with joy at having a chance to drink. I pulled my gear off and placed it all back in the order of which I removed it from my gear box. I pulled out a pack of cards and placed them on the table that Jonathan had put up in the room. I started cleaning my rifle while I waited for everyone to get back to play. I noticed my hands were a little shaky as I was trying to clean the finer points that required me to focus and hold steady. The steadier I tried to hold them the more my hands trembled.

I put my rifle down shook my hands real hard saying a few profanities then sat back down and finished cleaning my rifle. My hands shaking meant this place was getting to me and I was losing my nerve. When would it start affecting my aim? How long could I keep it under control? That was the real question. I didn't have long to think about it because Dave and Jonathan busted in the door with a loud chant that I didn't recognize. They both obviously had a few sips prior to getting here.

Chap walked in shortly after, took his seat, and started splitting up the chips. I snagged my seat and started shuffling the deck.

I passed two cards around to everyone. We started small and big blind. Chap called, and it went around the table everyone doing the same including me. I burned a card and revealed three. I didn't even have a pair at this point. Chap raised, Jonathan called. Dave and I folded. I had a sip from my flask and watched the rest of the hand play out as I dealt the flop and river. I pulled out a box from under my gear while Chap was shuffling the next hand.

I had secured some Cuban Cigars from a local a few days earlier. I passed one to everyone at the table. Dave and Jonathan yelled, "CHEERS!" We all lifted our flasks and took a swig. There was something extra relaxing about a good cigar and strong alcohol. It was almost as if nothing had happened before this moment and it felt like we were home for a while. It was moments like this I lived for. Chap continued to deal the hand, I folded again, and the other three played it out.

The game went back and forth for a while until it was just me and Chap left. Dave was passed out on my bunk and Jonathan was sprawled out on the floor. Chap was the dealer for this hand. As Chap was dealing the cards he said, "Look at those two light weights." I looked at Jonathan and Dave and laughed before talking, "Yeah, but they had fun and that was the point. If you work hard you deserve to play just as hard." Chap tried to blow Cigar smoke in my face as he spoke, "I raise you. This was Dave's last patrol he's going back to convoy and tower duty next week." I said as I blew Cigar smoke back at Chap, "I figured as much. I call. Our package pick up is the next patrol and I don't want anyone I know but you on that one."

Chap burned a card, turned three, and then spoke, "It's going to be a tight fit. Raise. And have you found a driver?" I frowned as I spoke, "No. There won't be another driver. Call. You are going to drive, I will man the gunner mount. You park, I get out and grab the package, and you man the mount. I return and we catch up to the evacuation team." Chap burned one and turned one before replying, "Sounds like a solid plan. Raise. I would like one extra body though." I smiled as I spoke. "Call. No extra body on this one. It's too dangerous. The less there is the better and, if anything goes down, we hightail it out and abandon the package."

Chap burned and turned the last two cards before talking again, "Raise. So what if that happens and we don't get the package?" I responded, "All in. Then I guess we both are in big trouble with Youssef. But I think his problem is bigger than ours. I have a feeling Youssef has a vested interest in seeing this package delivered. I also think he could provide some emergency back up without getting caught." Chap responded pushing all his chips in, "Calling your bluff. Once this is over I'm never playing for money again." I laughed as I showed a full house and spoke,

"I played like I had the straight and you must have a flush. Chap just shook his head as he spoke, "That's why I won't play for money anymore."

I laughed as I started putting the chips away, "You give away what you're thinking in your face and body language. It's all about reading people. It's no different than what I do when I'm assessing a person I'm about to speak to. You look at how their stance is and where they have decided to be positioned in the room. Anyone observant or defensive will be with their back to the corner and back straight. You look at their eyes: are they searching for something? Are they focused or random? Next look at the mouth: is there a smile, frown, or is it in between? This will give you a mood even if it is a false mood that is a sign as well. Then go to eyebrows and hands. If the eyebrows match the mouth in mood presentation: the mood is genuine. If not, then it's a false front. Are the hands steady or doing something? If so what are they doing? What they are doing is the final key. If they legitimately are doing something needed or wanted, then the person is occupied and won't notice a variety of movements or objects in peripheral vision. If the person is fidgeting with an object for example; rotating a pen or coin through their fingers. They are in thought or processing movements in the room and attempting to notice anyone approaching or looking for them."

Chap looked like he was deep in thought. I continued, "Those are the entry level observations that can help you win a game. Keep in mind others are doing this as well that have been playing the game for a while or have taken classes to learn about human behavior. The best people to play are the ones who don't know how to do this. They give away their hand without even knowing it also the people you know the best and are closest to you. There are less false signals that way. Body language is the best way to tell a person's true intentions. I use it all the time to send false signals to people who don't even know they are reading and reacting to it. You can manipulate a conversation without saying a word with the right body language. It's almost like a game, a dangerous game but a fun game. If you send the wrong body language it can ruin a conversation as well."

Chap started laughing and took a swig from the flask then spoke, "You've got too much time on your hands and that's too much work. I'll just say what I mean and the conversation goes where it will go." I laughed with him and replied, "I know pal, I don't use it with you just with people I don't know and when it is necessary such as in a poker game to win money." I elbowed him in the side as I said the last part. Chap laughed, downed the rest of his flask and lay down on the floor. I finished my flask and did the same. Sleep was overdue; I was still exhausted from the patrol.

# CHAPTER 8

Time seemed like it was at a standstill. I started to develop a hatred for this place. It was almost as if every time you turned around something was going wrong or ended bad. We were gearing up to go on one of the most dangerous extractions we have attempted up to date and I had a bad feeling. The information the informant had was extremely important and Chap was told to extract him at all costs. This usually meant several lives and lots of equipment wasted. Just as Chap and I were putting our gear in the HMMV our current situation turned worse. A new group of insurgents had been smuggled into the area from another country. Chap was told these guys were experienced in IED set up and had weapons training. Of course with the luck we were having they were supposedly in the village we had to drive through to get the informant and package.

I could tell Chap was a little stressed about the mission. We had been in danger before, but this was different. Usually, we were cocky and arrogant about going in. Death had been the norm up until now. It didn't bother me but I think risking Chap's life for an unknown package for an unknown person to get rid of debt he had put on himself was weighing on him. Maybe he was afraid to die on his own account or maybe he was afraid I would. I couldn't tell. I thought about talking to him about it but now we were leaving and it was a little late.

The extraction was going to be done in three teams. Chap and I had already discussed with everyone about our stop on the way back. They didn't know exactly what we were doing but they did know we would be separating at the end. Chap and I would play decoy for anyone in pursuit or would engage anyone in the way. This way everyone and the informant got to base quickly and we could snag the package on the way back. Chap and I planned on our HMMV taking a beating so we had a few plates added to the doors, grill, hood and fenders. I had layered the floor with sand bags and took out a 9mm pistol from the armory to go with my shot gun and rifle. I had given Dan a flask for the pistol and ammunition but I thought I won out on that end, you could never have enough fire power.

I learned quickly it was better to overdo it and live than underdo it and not make it. With the extra weight the HMMV seemed a little sluggish as we started to leave. I was more concerned with keeping it running and making it back than fuel consumption and acceleration at this point. Mission completion was a sure thing, but something about this one had me on edge with the new insurgents in the area. Not knowing how many or what they were used to doing was never a good thing.

Chap had brought on an extra Marine with us—even after I told him we shouldn't, but that was before we knew about the new threat. I felt more comfortable with an extra hand to shoot with us and was glad he didn't listen to me. The kid's name was Frank. I wasn't familiar with him but apparently, he was easy to bribe to keep quiet, and was good with his rifle. That was all the qualities I needed to know at the moment. Frank was a moderate size Marine, well built for patrols. I could tell he kept in good shape at the gym— his muscle tone showed even through his long sleeve shirt. I think he deliberately wore it a size too small to show off maybe.

The team passed through the gates of the base and headed towards our destination. When we got to the village it was dead silent. Normally people act like we're not there or there are so many kids you have to throw candy away from the vehicle for them to chase so you can keep moving. Something was wrong and everyone apparently knew except us. My face tingled and I had almost numbed my fingers from gripping the handle of the M249 SAW on the gunners mount so tight. When we exited the village, it was like a weight had lifted. I was sure we were going to be hit but nothing happened.

Still, I didn't like how no one was outside. Apparently neither did anyone else in the team. The radio chatter was nonstop about what we were going to possibly run into. Chap buzzed me on the private channel and started talking when I buzzed back that I switched. "I had eyes on the building we were going towards, our goal, it's a clear shot to it at the end. I estimate five minutes total time to get the package." I responded, "Sounds good should be simple once we break away. I have a feeling were going to have ample reasons to break away in that village. We've patrolled trough here many times and it has never been that empty on the streets."

Chap responded, "I agree they had someone relaying somehow we left the base going in this direction." I replied back, "Well we didn't get hit going in so they might be setting up a hit coming back. I suggest we change our return route to avoid and unwanted road blocks or IED's they could be laying. They know we have to return at some point—they just don't know when we will. I don't think they will plan on us changing our route." Chap responded, "I agree.

I will plan a new route back and relay the information and plan change." Chap and I switched back to the public channel. Chap was relaying the route change to the drivers as we stopped and the first team ran into the target building to extract the informant. They made it look like an infiltration and grab—zip tying him and putting a bag on his head. He even faked trying to escape and fought back. I was impressed. It looked very convincing, but we knew it was a rouse and he was our informant. They placed the informant in the second HMMV and we started to speed back to base on the secondary route we had planned. Once the building was out of view, we did a formation shuffle while we were driving, moving the informant from the second vehicle to the fourth.

We came to our first corner and took our alternate route. The streets were still empty and everyone was on edge. We continued on course and started taking light fire from the roof tops of several buildings but didn't stop. A stray round hit the M 249 SAW I was holding onto, damaging the cover. I said a few profanities as I pulled up my rifle and lowered the M249 SAW.

Our HMMV pulled away to distract and draw their fire as the extraction team continued. I fired a few rounds at the roof tops to keep the insurgents ducking for cover. Once the team called that they were clear of the last building. Frank floored it to the building with the package. I unclipped my shot gun and dropped my extra ammo to run faster when we stopped. As we stopped, I ran down the hood and into the building clearing rooms as I went to the roof. Chap was already in the gunners, mount with his rifle before I had even entered the building.

I got to the roof fairly quick, checking rooms as I went. Thank goodness the house was empty. I could see the package; it was a box about two feet long and a foot wide and weighed almost nothing. I snatched it up and ran back to the HMMV. I ran back up the hood and into the gunner's mount. Chap popped back inside to his seat and Frank floored it to rendezvous with the extraction team and back to base. Chap was off on his calculation that it only took three and a half minutes, but that just made it better. He started hooting and hollering as we caught up to the extraction team. I think he was overly relieved that it went so well.

I chucked to myself as we pulled into the base. All the planning and preparation, and the worst thing that happened were us getting peppered by a few stray rounds. Like I always say, 'It's better to be over prepared than under'. As the HMMV stopped I grabbed the package and motioned to Chap that I was off to deliver it. Chap just waived me off in acknowledgement and headed to debriefing with the informant.

I headed straight to Youssef's with the package. He was already outside his bunk house waiting for me and went inside when he saw me coming. I followed. He took the package from me as I walked in, passing me a slip of paper. It was a clearance buy-in note to hand to his dealer for Chaps debt. Once handed in, Chaps debt would be clear. Youssef put his hand on my shoulder to stop me as I was on my way out and said, "You could have asked for more and didn't, you knew this was dangerous but all you did was clear your friend's name. Why risk that much and not ask for more?" I lightly laughed as I brushed off his hand as I walked out and replied, "I have nothing to lose in my death. I have everything to gain in helping a friend." I headed to the debriefing room to find Chap. I arrived just as the debriefing had finished. Everyone was leaving the room; Chap was still looking at the map and pushing red pins into it, indicating more insurgent activity and locations. He looked up, saw me and smiled as he said, "That went a lot better than I could have hoped. With everything going wrong, I thought for sure it was going to be a bad run." I replied, "Sometimes you get lucky. Let's hand the buy note in and celebrate." Chap laughed and smiled as he followed me out the debriefing room.

We found the dealers bunk house and walked in. The dealer was an officer who was a bit older than we were, but looked as if he hadn't left the wire a day in his life. Chap passed him the note. The dealer grabbed the debt card out of his record book and handed it to Chap. He looked at it for a moment then put it in his pocket. As we walked out the door, I could see Chap seemed a lot more relaxed than he had been in a while and I was happy for him. Overcoming an addiction is not easy when you still have an ongoing issue because of it, in this case: debt. I think it becomes harder when the debt is a constant reminder.

Chap and I stopped and filled both our flasks on the way back to our bunks. We walked in and both went through our routine of stripping our gear, putting everything into its own specific place. I took off my t-shirt to put on something cleaner to relax in. Chap looked at me and said, "It looks like your injuries didn't scar." I ran my fingers across a few still visible marks on my chest and said, "I think they'll be gone by the time we get home." I started to get a headache as I thought about how I got them in the first place so I took a sip from my flask and changed the subject, "Lets burn your card as a starter in our celebration tonight."

Chap pulled the card out of his pocket and stared at it, then said, "No, I think I'll keep it as a reminder to stay away from playing without friends." I laughed as I said, "I'd just as soon forget the whole damn thing." Chap patted me on the back as he took another sip from his flask. He sat down across from me in a chair. I pulled up my chair and sat as well. The two of us sat there in silence just sipping from our flasks and starring at nothing. I'm not sure what Chap was thinking, but I was just enjoying the peacefulness of our room and an end to my buddy's debt.

The quiet didn't last too long. The mosque started playing prayer music like clockwork. I just put in my ear plugs and pulled out two cigars, handing one to Chap. He gave me an exaggerated false salute as he lit his and leaned over to light mine. I puffed the cigar slow enough to enjoy it and make it last, but enough to keep it lit. I've learned over time, if you go too slowly, it burns out and ruins the taste when you relight it. The nicotine sent a warm feeling to my gut as it mingled with the buzz from the alcohol. Chap almost looked like he was asleep if it wasn't for the fact he was puffing the cigar every now and then.

Chap didn't even bother to ash. He just let it fall on his shirt and lap as he sat, enjoying the feeling of the two habits working together. I thought about the events of the day and still couldn't figure why we weren't attacked—every report said we would get hit hard. No one gets as lucky as we did in a hot zone. Maybe when we rerouted, we really threw them off. Maybe they weren't ready to attack who knows. I'm just glad it went as well as it did. I had almost finished my flask just as I finished my thoughts on the extraction.

I could see Chap has finally passed out, cigar in mouth and flask in hand still. I grabbed his cigar and made sure it was out and did the same to mine. I put our flasks away and sat back in the chair. I let my mind wander around a bit. I was thinking about home and family, and then about how much I hated this place and the people who lived here. I didn't feel this way at the beginning and I couldn't stomach how they treated their women and children. It was a shock the first time you see a man beat his family, but it became a regular sight and you just had to ignore it. I think I just hated the fact that I couldn't help them due to political restrictions on what we were allowed to get involved in.

I fell asleep pretty fast after my mind wandered too much. I woke up in the morning to Chap kicking my boot to get my attention. He spoke as I woke up, "Let's go." The morning run went the same as any other day. We ran. I got sick, and then Chap got sick, and then we changed and went to breakfast. Same thing: day-in and day-out. Nothing had changed other than where we were going during patrol and what we were doing on patrol. At this point we weren't living; we were just surviving and doing our job.

After breakfast we returned back to the bunk house. Everything seemed normal, mortars raining down as usual. Chap and I didn't even flinch or hesitate in step. We just kept walking. The next thing was the wailing of the siren and more mortars. Everything was the same. Then, something was out of place, gun fire during the day from a tower! This was normal at night but it had never happened at daytime before. Chap gave me a puzzled and confused look and we both turned toward the sound of the gun fire.

More weapons chimed in with the sound of the first.

There came a few small explosions and then a bigger explosion. Chap had a panicked look on his face as he spoke, "That's Dave's tower and he's on duty!" Chap broke into a sprint to the tower and I was right behind him. The explosions and mortars stopped, but the gunfire continued. When we got to the tower and saw that part of the top looked like it had caved in from a mortar impact. There was smoke but no fire. Both of us rushed up the stairs to get to the top. The door had too much debris behind it to open. We could see someone was trapped and not moving and were now franticly trying to open the door.

Chap started butt stroking the hinge on the door to break it, but it was no use. I yelled to Chap, "We'll have to run across from the other tower." Both of us sprinted back down the stairs to the opposite tower on the other side of the back gate. We rushed up the tower stairs and started climbing through the window at the top onto the wall. It was wide enough that we could still almost sprint. I could hear bullets coming close to us as we ran to the other tower. We obviously made good targets and we didn't have on our armor! I practically dove into the window to avoid getting shot. Chap followed, landing on top of me. I quickly rolled him off and saw the rubble on Dave. In a panic, Chap and I started moving the rubble and unbarring him. By the time the rubble was clear it was too late.

Once I realized that Dave was gone, I also noticed the shooting had finally stopped. A medic came through the window shortly after and checked Dave's pulse, calling his death over his head set. The doc tried to get Chap to let go but he wouldn't release him.

Chap just sat there holding Dave close crying. I pulled the doc away from Chap and shook my head 'No.' The Doc just patted me on the back and went back through the window. I had tears rolling down my cheeks as I looked at the scene in front of me. I had no words to offer in loss, and no words to say in comfort. As Chap was still holding Dave I reached around Dave's neck and removed his dog tags. I put them in my pocket and picked both Chap and Dave up. I finally spoke, "Let's get him out of the tower."

I went through the window first and Chap passed me Dave. I put him over my shoulder and walked to the other tower. Chap went past me and through the window and I passed Dave to him. Chap had Dave in a fireman's carry as he went down the stairs of the tower. When we got to the bottom of the tower I could see Jonathan had come to see if Dave was alright. Jonathan's face drained of color. He turned and left when he saw Chap carrying Dave.

Chap set Dave down against the wall and sat beside him and lit a cigarette. He put it in Dave's lips so it wouldn't fall and lit another for himself. I lit a cigarette as I told the bystanders to leave us alone. I think Chap had been mentally broken now. He was having a full blown one way conversation with Dave as if he was talking back to him. I can't blame him for losing it. I think I was only keeping it together because Chap wasn't.

They finally came to take Dave's body. I had to help them hold down Chap—I think he was still in denial. After tussling for a bit, I got my bicep around Chaps neck and blood choked him until he passed out. I waited until he woke up and tried to help him up but he brushed my hand out of the way. I figured he would come to terms with what happened eventually. I just left him alone and followed where ever he was walking to.

I followed far enough behind so that he didn't really notice. I was a little worried about what he might do. Normally I was the rash one but it's almost as if Chap and I had traded places when we got here. The longer we were here the more dangerous Chap became and the more cautious I became. I didn't even interact with anyone anymore except Chap, Dave and Jonathan. Now that

Dave was gone, it was one less person I was willing to interact with on a personal level. Chap ended up at Dave's bunk house. I could see Jonathan was there as well. He was my friend as well, but I wasn't about to lose my emotions—it would be too dangerous. I was angry and I wanted to stay that way for now. I didn't like losing emotions; they made me feel weak and helpless. Maybe I was in denial of how I felt, but I wasn't ready to talk about Dave. Chap and Jonathan talked for over an hour as I watched. Chap seemed like he had calmed down so I decided to head back to the bunk and drink.

I filled my flask, took a big swig twice, and topped the flask up again. I choked and started coughing, it was almost too strong for me to drink that much that fast. I'm not sure on how strong my batches were. All I knew was one flask was more than enough to do me in. Back home I could easily drink three quarters of a 750ml bottle of Jack or Jim. Sometimes the whole bottle depending on how long I nursed it.

By the time I sat in my chair at my bunk I was pretty drunk. I had turned to drinking for a lot of things. I went to set my flask on the table and my hand was trembling so much I almost spilled it. I tried to force myself to hold it steady but it only shook worse. I had been getting the trembles more often and they were getting more visible as well. I had nerves of steel on the battle field but as soon as I would relax my body would give in.

I started getting angry again, why couldn't I control my own hands? What is wrong with my muscles? Why they won't listen? I want them to steady but they won't. I continued drinking as I argued with myself about what might be wrong. I thought, maybe it was a disease from this place in hell, maybe my mind is broken and this is a symptom, or maybe it's just the stress. I kept listing things and trying to convince myself it was nothing. I had to hold it in and show no weakness, for that would be my undoing.

I could feel myself passing out and forced

myself to take another drink. I started to think about Dave. All he wanted to do was get some action. Make his trip worthwhile. All I wanted to do was drop napalm on this place we all called Hell and go home. Why we were here? We were here to make peace for a people who didn't want it. We all knew as soon as we leave it was going back to the way it was. There was no real reason to be here. My thoughts faded as I passed out.

# CHAPTER 9

A few weeks had gone by since Dave passed away. I can barely remember what all we did. Time seemed to just slip away from all of us. Chap drowned himself in patrols and I think Jonathan has been avoiding me. I tried to find him once or twice, but I guess he found new places to hide. He didn't seem to stay in one place long enough for me to catch up with him. I didn't want to bother him at his post—it would have been awkward. It was time for another patrol run in about an hour, not leaving me too much time to goof around. I had to go get ready once again; it all just seemed emotionless at this point. This feeling is a dangerous place to be. Chap was already at the bunk and geared up when I got there. As I came in he tossed me his empty flask as to say 'Better make more.' I set the flask in my gear box and started getting ready. I had gotten ready faster than usual and had some time to spare. I sat in my chair and reached in my grenade pouch. I don't think Chap noticed but I had been collecting dog tags from the ones that didn't make it with us. I had quite the collection. But I wasn't sure exactly why I was collecting them.

I started keeping these dog tags with Jeff's death in the tower. I didn't even remember taking it, but I had it in my grenade pocket ever since then. Every time someone we were with died, I collected their dog tag and kept it with Jeff's as to keep him company, I suppose. When I collected Dave's dog tags it helped me from getting out of control. It made me feel as if I am saying I will remember, you will not be forgotten. I had collected two more since Dave passed and thus far, I had eight. It didn't seem like a lot, but to us it was.

I wasn't even sure what I was going to do with them all when I got back home. I thought about visiting the families and seeing what their personal lives were like—if they had any family. Not to interact with any of them, but just to observe and see who was missed and who left something important undone. I thought maybe I could help with the undone tasks. I didn't get too much into the rest of the thought as I found myself at the HMMV. Chap was yelling for me at the front of the first HMMV.

Chap was going over the layout of the village. This patrol was an unplanned one. Chap had gotten intel that several of the new insurgents in the area were in the town today with arms and Russian artillery rounds. The artillery rounds were always used as IED's. It paid to know what they possibly brought. It gave us an idea of how deadly the blast could potentially be. The Russian rounds were not very nice as an IED. The blast was usually enough to tear through an HMMV easily if done properly, maiming or killing the soldiers in it.

We all got into the HMMV's, the patrols were straight forward: clear the buildings and attempt to capture any insurgents alive for interrogation. We headed out on what was going to be a longer drive than usual. The village we were going to was on the very outer edge of the zone in our patrol. We had been coordinating with an army armored division for assistance and support. We wouldn't get any help from our base—it would take too long. We went through several villages along the way.

Kids were coming up to the HMMV, I'd toss candy a few feet from the road and they would scatter like little spiders to pick them all up. The candy wasn't really for them; it was to get them away from the vehicle. If they got too close it would slow us down and make us a target for snipers. The mother of the children said something to them loudly and the kids bolted inside leaving the rest of the candy. I spoke on the head piece for the convoy to hear, "Locals going inside in a panic. Keep your eyes open."

Not too long after I spoke, pop shots from

a sniper started flying by the patrol. This was one of the only things I hated about being a gunner. I was the only damn target on the vehicle worth shooting at. I searched the building tops but couldn't see anything. Maybe he was shooting through a window—it was hard to tell. It didn't matter we were gaining distance and his aim was poor. If that was me, I would have been able to pick off all the gunners in our patrol by now. I am not complaining—I am thankful that they can't shoot the broad side of a barn. It was usually luck when they did hit someone and I doubt they usually hit what they were aiming at.

I had been shot at more times than I could count. I learned that I had time to aim and shoot at whatever was shooting at me, so long as they were farther than 100 yards. If they were closer, you would need cover. Even a child could hit something closer than 100 yards if unloading a whole magazine. I was glad to be out of firing range and on the road to the last village to seek our target. It was a decent drive. We weren't even at the village yet and over an hour had passed. I was on edge because we were going in a little blind. Normally we plan for a day or two how the patrol is going to play out. I felt uncomfortable about this one because we only had a few hours' notice. Planning is vital and most of that time was spent getting our gear ready. We always had emergency plans but they never took into account possible fall back locations or how to route the insurgents through the buildings to trap them. We did have a plan, but I just wasn't comfortable with not being able to work out the 'What if?' scenarios.

We stopped prior to the village and got out. Chap had organized it like one of our previous patrols. The HMMV's would circle around and assist where needed, while the ground patrol cleared the buildings from front to back. It was a solid plan. The only problem was these were different insurgents and more organized. Plus, this area wasn't as square as the village prior. Given the short amount of time we had, it was the best plan all of us could come up with. The HMMV's took Chap and me, along with two other Marines towards the left side. There were two center squads clearing that area and then one on the right. There were sixteen in total taking the ground with six HMMV's with a driver and gunner each circling the village. Our group didn't get too far into the first house before we could hear gunfire from multiple locations. Chatter over the head set said where and approximately how many there were. Chap stopped us to coordinate vehicles to the locations and then we continued to clear the house.

We got to the top room of the building. This house was clear but it was evident that the insurgents had been here. The mother and two kids were in the corner huddled together in their final position. The father was tied up to a chair hanging life less facing the family. The father had a single shot to the head but the family looked like they took the full magazine from an AK47. By the smell they had been dead for at least two days. It was enough to make us pause for a second at the brutal carnage inflicted by the insurgents before we continued.

I heard both the other Marines with us mumble a few profanities about the scene as we left. Chap and I said nothing we just kept moving. The sound of random gunfire never stopped. Every time it was from a different location that was called in. They were good at what they were doing but we were better. It didn't matter how they fought they would die or get captured. The only thing that changed was how many we might lose or have injured. I could see a tear in Chaps eye as he pushed us harder and faster to clear the houses to where the action was. I think the sight of the family got to him. He was more determined to have our route done so we could box the insurgents in.

We cleared the last house on our section and began sweeping in, tightening the circle on available houses the insurgents could get to. They must have had quite a bit in the village. They had already taken more than a dozen losses and still had enough to keep us moving slow. The two Marines with Chap and I had been ahead of us by about three feet, clearing the whole way. I was impressed with their efficiency. One would go left the other right and Chap and I cleared center and roof. It was a smooth system.

As we were clearing the second floor of another house, we could hear footsteps up top. We were just about at the stairs and had one room left to clear. As soon as the two Marines went in, I could hear one of them barley yell out to get back. The room lit up in an explosion, coming out the door and throwing one of the Marines against the opposite wall. I narrowly got to turn and duck as the wall beside Chap and I blew into us. It was as if time had slowed. I could see everything collapsing into us and feel the heat on my uncovered skin, then the compression on my whole body as I got thrown with the debris like a rag doll.

I regained consciousness and was choking on smoke. My ears were still ringing from the blast. I scrambled to get the debris off me and get my rifle ready. I felt pain all over from the blast, mostly on my left side. I couldn't hear anything but the ringing. I knew the insurgents on the roof knew we were here now. I tried to raise my rifle but my hands were shaking too much to hold steady. So I propped my rifle up on the debris and went prone watching the stairwell. Sure enough, two insurgents came down. I was unsure how many were up top. I waited until they were at the second landing as to block the way. I fired one burst of three rounds each and they dropped onto the landing.

I struggled to get back up and went to the rubble trying to find Chap. I tried shouting for him, but I wasn't sure if he wasn't responding or if I still couldn't hear over the ringing in my ears. Finally, I found his boot and foot was sticking out from a fairly large section of the wall that had collapsed on him. I looked to find a way to lift it off without injuring him—if he was still alive. I had to guess at how he was facing and laying. I couldn't be sure so I lifted parallel to the boot, hoping his leg wasn't twisted in the wrong direction. As I lifted, Chap scrambled to get out from underneath. He seemed to be ok. He was yelling something at me and I realized he must have been hollering the whole time—I just couldn't hear it. Chap pulled out his pistol and fired a few rounds. I turned around and tried to aim but the target was already down. He started yelling at me but I couldn't hear what he was saying, I just pointed at my ears and shook my head. All I could see was his arm flapping around as he was talking. I think he figured out that I couldn't hear and assumed he was yelling profanities about the situation.

He motioned for me to follow him. We checked the two dead Marines as we passed. One was lying on the floor in the hallway. He had flash burns on his gear and skin. It looked bad. I felt for a pulse knowing there would not be one and then shut his eyes. I grabbed his dog tags and moved over to the other Marine. It was hard to tell that he used to be a Marine, minus the gear and weapon. I didn't have to get any closer to see if he survived—it was obvious he didn't make it. I grabbed the bloodstained dog tags and returned to Chap, shaking my head no. Chap understood and we headed to the stairs. I could see Chap was gritting his teeth as we headed up the stair well. Chap popped onto the roof fast without looking, He was quick enough on the trigger to drop both the insurgents that were remaining up there. I could see he was talking on his head set and was coordinating the rest of the group. I started taking out targets on the roof tops of lower buildings that still hadn't been cleared while he was on the head set.

The ringing started to subside. I started to hear muffled sounds but still, everything wasn't fully audible. I could see several buildings were smoking now. Whatever we came across, several other squads must have as well. Those must have gone on while my hearing was lost because I never heard them prior to ours. Chap had called something on the head set and motioned me to go down. I picked up the dog tags from the two Marines and put one of them on my shoulder. Chap carried the other and we proceeded to leave the building.

Once we got to the bottom floor and out the door a HMMV was waiting for us. The driver loaded the two dead Marines and drove off. Chap signaled at me to follow him so I did. I was relying on his hearing, but I still had my sight and rifle. As long as I could see, we were good. A few of the other buildings must have been cleared because Chap skipped them and went a few houses down and met up with another squad.

He communicated with their squad leader and we proceeded to clear rooms again. I was still shouting calls like, 'All Clear!' as I moved through the rooms, but I could only hear low muffled tones. I could hear Chap saying the commands but not enough to hear what he was saying. I didn't need to hear it exactly anyway—we had done it enough that I knew what the sounds were. I just had to stick to my training which had become second nature.

We cleared the house and headed out back to the next one when my hearing had almost come back. I could hear Chap still communicating as if I could hear him the whole time. Only now I could understand what he was saying. The adrenaline from the blast was wearing off and I could feel several things weren't right in my body, but I wasn't sure what they were. I would pivot fast and a sharp pain in my spine would run up to my neck. I wasn't sure how bad it was, but we had to finish here before I could figure out what I needed.

I could hear the gunfire still going from multiple engagements. The ground kept shaking from the armor from the Army, meaning they must be helping us. It must have gotten pretty bad, I figured, to ask the armor for assistance. As we came out of the house I saw an M1A1 with a loose track. It looked like it hit and IED and decided to just stay put—it was a tank, it could sit where ever it wanted and be fine. Even an RPG wouldn't do much but scratch the paint. It was made to take impacts from other tanks. An artillery round to the treads would do a good job at making it immobile for a while though.

I Followed Chap, realizing he was pretty injured as well. I could see a blood stain that had started on his left shoulder was now run down his entire arm was dripping on the ground. My knee almost buckled on me a few times as we continued trying to clear. I wondered how many spots I had like that but I decided not to check quite yet.

We had created a bottle neck with only two houses left to be searched. The remaining insurgents were in them and Chap put the interpreter on the loud speaker to try and get them to give up. They only responded with fire so we started to clear both buildings at the same time. I sat this one out at the

HMMV—too many going in to clear and I would only get in the way. I watched the windows for anything I could shoot at. The insurgents no longer cared about what was going on outside the building now that they were being attacked from the inside.

I could hear the gun fire and see flashes in each window as the Marines cleared the rest of the house. It didn't take more than five minutes to have the house clear. I looked at our HMMV and could see it had taken fire as well while it was circling the village. It looked like a few insurgents had surrendered earlier. They were zip tied and in the back of a few of the HMMV's. I half wished we hadn't taken any survivors but the intel they would provide usually saved lives in the long run. It was worth putting up with.

Chap had a doc attending him at the lead HMMV now that everything was over. I climbed into the HMMV and waited for us to leave. I was sore and tired and had enough death for today. Hopefully with this insurgent threat gone from this zone things would slow down and we could take a longer break. Going home wasn't far from now and I was ready to go. You never plan anything for home until you're close to leaving. You experience enough loss that you tend to just stay in the moment and not plan ahead—just in case you happen not to make it.

I didn't put much more thought into it before Chap opened the door. He dragged me out of the HMMV so the doc could look me over. The doc made some comment about medium concussion and possible hearing loss from ear drum damage. I hadn't even realized I had bled from my ears until the doc cleaned it up. The doc picked a few wood splinters and rocks out of my lower left side of my back from the blast I had sustained and made sure nothing was bleeding to badly then left.

I lightly laughed as Chap looked at me. "What's so funny?" Chap said. I responded, "I bet we look like a pair. You look like you went to hell and back." Chap smirked as he spoke, "Only to kill the devil." I smiled back and we both got in the HMMV. The patrol was packed and ready to leave. From what I could gather we had six wounded, counting Chap and I, and three lost. The mood was a little grim heading back but we had completed what we came out to do and with several detainees that could give important information to an interrogator.

We came to the small village we were at before that had the sniper. The street was completely clear this time. All of the sudden the lead HMMV hit an IED. I could feel the wave from the blast even from three vehicles back. The HMMV's front end had practically gone vertical in the air and fell sideways to the ground. Several insurgents from the roof tops started firing. We returned fire to suppress them.

The second HMMV pulled in front of the first and the Marines scrambled to get the guy out and into their HMMV. Still under fire and the gunners engaging targets the Marines hooked the first HMMV to the second at the back and got in and started dragging the wreckage behind them. We didn't stop until we were out of sight of the village. Once it was clear we stopped and assessed the damage. We couldn't drag it the whole way.

We used the manual winches we had for emergencies like these to lift the back end and connect it to our HMMV so it could roll on its rear wheels. We reconnected what was left of the front to the other HMMV. Now that just one HMMV wasn't struggling to move the damaged one we continued to base. It seemed the driver and other Marines in that vehicle were okay just a little shaken up. Chatter was going back and forth on the head set. There were so many profanities a normal person wouldn't have understood the conversation.

We got back to the base to meet several docs waiting to examine all of us and a few Marines to take the detainees to interrogation. I did a pretty good job of ducking anyone trying to talk to or examine me and left for my bunk. I got several long stares from people on the base as they looked at the condition of me and my gear. My front sappy plate was almost hanging out. Rips were everywhere on all my clothes and gear. I still had blood on my face, sleeves, and on the back left of my gear and shirt. I had so much soot and dirt on me you almost couldn't tell I had proper camouflage clothes on. I didn't even go into the bunk house I just sat down and put my back against it. At this point I didn't care about anything. I just wanted a rest and to be alone for a bit. I knew eventually Chap would send a Doc after me but I was hoping he was too busy to do it in a timely manner. There was something comforting and soothing about being in my gear. I felt safe and secure. I closed my eyes and let myself drift to sleep as I started to relax.

I'm not sure how long I was asleep but Chap kicked me awake. I was still so sore that it hurt worse than usual. I looked up and saw the Doc with him. The Doc checked my dressings on my back and made sure all my limbs and fingers moved properly. He asked if I had blurred vision or was nauseous. I told him no. The Doc told Chap I was fit enough for duty and left. Chap sat down beside me and lit two cigarettes and passed me one. We just sat there smoking not saying anything. Chap spoke up after the third smoke, "I hate this place." "We all do," I replied. "We nick named it hell for a reason. It's hot as hell, it's boring as hell, it's dangerous as hell, and everyone we kill here goes to hell." Chap started to chuckle as he spoke, "I thought all Marines go to hell to take over." I responded, "When I die, I would rather guard the gate but if you charge into hell, you know I will charge in with you. The real place couldn't be any worse than being here anyway.

Chap just patted my back and got up of the ground. He paused for a moment then helped me up and we both went into the bunk house. Chap grabbed both our flasks and left to go fill them. I was hungry but I was too lazy to take off my gear let alone going to the chow hall. I pulled the MRE I had in my pack out. It was jambalaya which sounds good unless you've had it before. The novelty of MRE's wears off after your first field training. Once you eat them for a few days you learn which ones to avoid and which ones to take. The question is, 'Why eat them unless you have to?'

I thought about eating it for a moment then decided I wasn't hungry enough and put it back in my pack and waited for Chap. He was taking longer than usual, so I finally decided to take my gear off. I put what was usable into my gear box where it belonged. Then I put what was not reusable in a pile on the floor. I would have to take it all in to see Dan and get new gear now that most of mine was ruined.

I was wondering why my back was so sore until I pulled out my half shattered sappy plate. It was together, but cracked and flimsy and not solid the way it was supposed to be.

I could see where the round hit it. I don't recall being shot though. Not sure how I missed being shot in the back. I got lucky; it was almost dead center in the plate. I picked up my pack and could see where it went in. it looked like it hit my pack went through my extra clothes and into my sappy plate.

Chap finally came in with the flasks. I figured out on my own what took him so long—he stopped to grab smokes. As hungry as we both were, it didn't take long for the alcohol to kick in after we started drinking. After a while, several other Marines on the patrol joined us in the bunk—Chap must have invited them to share the alcohol. I wasn't overly impressed, I just wanted to be alone but it seemed to make Chap content so I tolerated it.

Those poor guys did not know what they were drinking. Before Chap and I knew it, we had several passed out, drunken Marines on our floor and racks. I should have grabbed my bunk when I had the chance, because we were stuck sleeping in our chairs. Chap looked at me with a smile as he leaned back to go to sleep. I fake saluted and downed the rest of my flask. I tried to drown my thoughts out and quiet my mind, but it was getting harder and harder to be calm enough to sleep. Once the alcohol hit its peak I surrendered to passing out.

# CHAPTER 10

My hand tremors had been getting worse of late. I initially thought it was the drinking, but when I had stopped drinking, they didn't get any better. To make matters even worse Chap thought something was wrong because I wasn't drinking with him anymore. I don't know why, but I just couldn't talk to Chap about it. I was supposed to be the strong one that carried us through. A lot of people at this point had been relying on me for not only the alcohol, but advice, or someone just to vent on or talk to.

I think Chap was even worse off than me. You couldn't wake him up without being attacked. I had been waiting a while for Chap to wake up as my mind wondered through various thoughts. I had been worried about him lately. He had been getting more aggressive and talking to himself. His night terrors had turned into what deemed 'sleeping combat'. Chap had been constantly in combat situations and now it was in his dreams while sleeping too. Attempting to wake him up had become dangerous.

I had found that if I poked him with a broom handle, I would be far enough away that he would come to his senses before fully engaging me. Chap had cut me a few times before—I was fairly better than him in a fight, but attempting to subdue him while he was going all out was difficult. Everyone else refused to approach him if he fell asleep (he put another Marine that woke him up in the infirmary). When we tried to do something, like telling the Officers about our situation, it was just swept it under the table. Maybe it was because we just couldn't afford to lose anyone as we were already shorthanded as it was. Who knows why we really could not get any help, the point remains that we didn't.

Chap still hadn't woken up and I was getting hungry. I decided I wasn't going to wait any longer and grabbed the broom handle. I attempted to yell him awake but he had his ear plugs in to block the mosque music. I poked him in the side with the broom. At least he was predictable due to training. Chap tried to arm bar whatever poked him and came out with the knife in a low jab, but nothing was there. I could see by the look in his eyes as he came at me, he still wasn't aware of his surroundings or who I was.

He lunged at me with the blade in a perfectly executed knife jab, just like we had been trained. Fortunately for me I was just a bit faster and better at it. I deflected the blade by wrapping my loose shirt sleeve around it and pulled Chap's arm over my shoulder, throwing him with a hip toss. He slammed into the floor and I knew he had come around when he said a few profanities. Chap got off the floor and sat in his chair in silence. To lighten the mood, I just smiled at him and said, "Let's go eat."

Chap followed me out of the bunk and into

the chow hall without arguing. I could tell it was bothering him that he had attacked me again. I knew he wanted to apologize but I think he was too embarrassed that he had lost control of his actions. I knew how he felt because I was feeling it too. Lost and confused. We did everything right, just like we were trained: we survived and the enemy did not, we followed the rules (for the most part), and yet our minds were betraying us. It had become a daily struggle to keep it together. I found as long as I kept us busy, our minds didn't have time to play tricks on our senses.

Chap and I sat quiet through breakfast. My tastes had changed since coming here and a lot of things that used to be my favorites no longer were. It was frustrating. I tried to force myself to eat the things I used to like but it got to the point I would almost gag as if my body was rejecting it. I used to be social and help people. I used to acquire things for fun or to aide others. Now I found myself a recluse who spent time just with Chap. I hadn't even seen Jonathan in a while. What is happening to me? Can I even speculate at this point?

Chap ate his breakfast faster than usual and didn't say anything to me as he got up to leave. I figured I would let him have some alone time and maybe he would want to talk later. To be honest I wanted a little personal space anyway. I finished up the yogurt I was eating and left as well. There were no more patrols for us to go on. We were heading home in two days. Our remaining time was supposed to be spent prepping to go home and getting everything decent enough for the Marines replacing us.

I headed to the phone booths to contact my family and give them approximate dates when I was going home. They seemed eager and excited to see me and I was happy to see them, but not as excited as I should have been. I knew the first trip home would be filled with potentially awkward questions and answers I wasn't willing to share. I knew they would say that they understood, but I knew they couldn't. That was just a basic response anyone makes in that situation.

I talked to them for a while. It didn't feel like long, but I had used almost all my phone cards so it must have been over an hour. I headed back to my bunk. I had to sell or disassemble the still I had made. I had already given Dan all the extra weapons he had loaned me for the deployment. There were a few people trying to smuggle goods back home in our gear quad cons, everyone seemed to be turning a blind eye to it. It almost looked like everyone had something they were trying to bring back.

I didn't want anything from this place. I just wanted to forget and go home. There was some jewelry I had acquired that I was going to give to my family, but other than that nothing seemed worth remembering.

I found Chap in the bunk house sorting his gear and had already taken apart the still. Chap spoke as he packed, "Orders from above were to pack our gear and keep one magazine of ammo for the trip, nothing extra on your person." I had already packed my gear last night so I was good to go. As I sat down, I spoke, "I'm heading to see my family when we get back, I'm not sure what your family is doing or where you're going but you can join me if you like."

Chap kept packing as he talked, "I'll think about it. I'm not sure what I'm going to do for my 30 days leave yet. I just want to be away from everything for a while I think." I replied, "Sounds like a plan. You can join me anytime in-between. The offer stays open." I waited until Chap was done packing. We both headed to the quad cons to drop our gear for transit.

As Chap put his pack in the quad con, he looked at me and said, "I got a letter a few days ago from my girlfriend. Now that I'm coming home, she no longer wants me to send her money, and she doesn't want to be with me." I could see her betrayal hurt all over Chap's face as he spoke and suggested, "She couldn't have just decided that."

Chap spoke again, "No. I think she tricked me from the beginning and took advantage of the fact I was leaving for a long time. I have been thinking about the reasons for a while and how I felt about the whole thing." I put my hand on his shoulder, "Sorry bro. I knew something was bothering you more than usual lately. I just wasn't sure what it was. When we get home, I'll take you out. On me. It'll be a blast."

Chap looked at me and smiled slightly as he said, "You don't have to spend money on me, but having a night out on the town with you like we use to sounds like fun." We continued back to our bunks to get the rest of our gear that we were traveling with.

As we walked in, I looked at the dismantled still and spoke. "I'm going to miss our free alcohol. I feel almost like we are leaving a friend behind." Chap replied, "Yeah but it's back to base life for now and it belongs here for someone else to reassemble and use. It's helped us. Now hopefully it will help someone else. I don't know how we would have coped without it." I laughed and said, "We just would have gone crazier than we already have I don't think too much would have changed."

Chap shrugged his shoulders and spoke, "I still think it helped." I ignored his last comment on the topic and grabbed my stuff. Even though we were leaving in two days, we had to leave our bunk house today. Our replacements were coming in around lunch time and were moving into the bunks right away when they got here. We were going to have to sleep outside, or in the 7 tons that had come in yesterday that were taking us on the first leg of our trip home. It was almost as if the insurgents knew we were going home soon. Mortar attacks had increased quite a bit today. Normally it had been one or two every few days lately but for some reason since we got up this morning there had already been six.

Chap spoke as we were walking to see the new Marines coming on the base at the main gate. "How do you think they know we are leaving and our replacements are coming?" I shrugged my shoulders as I responded, "Maybe the informant's trade information for both sides. Maybe they hear our phone conversations home. I doubt they know for sure." Chap responded, "Think about it: we got mortars when we got here, our convoy got attacked picking us up, mortars are raining down way more than usual, we leave tomorrow, and our replacements get here today. They have to know somehow." I paused in thought for a moment before speaking, "I see your point, but I doubt they know for sure. The leak is probably from the locals that the base hires to sweep the streets for us. It's charity to help them, but I bet that's where the information leaks from."

Chap paused and looked at the two locals in front of us pushing the brooms and said, "That is such an endless and pointless task and a waste of time because the sand and dust are everywhere. Why don't they pay them to fill sand bags for our barricades or something useful?" I laughed as I responded, "Like I said, it is charity work to put money back into their community. It isn't meant to be hard work. Just some busy work that we can pay them for."

Chap just grumbled under his breath then spoke up, "Why don't they put the money to good use and help us out? We get paid so little, even after coming here and not spending any money for six months that I still can't afford a decent place to live off-base." I spoke up, "Living in the barracks isn't that bad. It's free. You have free food three times a day. The gym is free, the recreational building is free, and a decent beach spot is only a thirty minute drive."

Chap smiled as he spoke, "Yeah, I do miss being on base compared to here. You're right. I'm just so angry at everything lately. I don't know what's going on. Usually, I have the good Ideas and you have the bad ones and are the one complaining. I just don't feel like myself anymore. I want how I used to feel to come back." Saddened, I looked at the floor as I said, "I know what you mean. I've tried, but I don't even like the same food any more. I'm me, but I'm not. I want to care about things I used to care about, but I can't seem to care anymore. All I feel is this growing anger. It's as if things are just not right about almost everything."

Chap put his hand on my shoulder and said, "Whatever is going on, we'll get through it together. I'm glad you're still here with me." I lightened up and almost smiled and said, "I'm glad we came together." Chap started laughing as he spoke, "I told you I had to come to make sure you came home. I didn't want you out here alone. Who knows what you would have gotten yourself into?" I laughed and replied, "Yeah. You saved me more than a few times. I'll give you that."

As we finished talking the convoy with our replacements came through the gate. We watched as they drove by. Chap spoke up as we watched the seven tons and HMMV's, "I told you the insurgents knew. Their convoy got hit too." I looked at all the shot marks and impacts the vehicles had taken almost everyone had some sort of damage. I spoke up, "Well, looks like they made it through intact. Guess that's what we have to look forward to tomorrow afternoon." Chap didn't seem impressed as he spoke, "We didn't come this far to be on our way home and get knocked off." I pulled Chaps arm to get him to follow me as I spoke, "I'm sure we'll be fine. Sure, we will get shot at maybe an IED or two but at the end of the day we will be on a C-130 and on our way to Camp Lejeune. By this time a few days from now, we will be drinking in a bar or already passed out on the floor." Chap chuckled as he spoke, "Maybe you'll be passed out. I plan on enjoying every moment of being completely intoxicated. I'll probably be doing something stupid that you came up with while you were drinking like we used to."

Chap and I left the conversation at that and headed to the chow hall for lunch. When I first came here I usually ate a salad and fruit, then maybe a sandwich or two. Now I was all about steak, cheese and potatoes. I didn't even like looking at salad anymore, let alone eating it. I was all about filling my plate full of vegetables, salad, and to top it off with cheese, bacon bits, chopped ham, and ranch dressing. Now all I wanted was a medium rare to rare steak with some sauce and a pile of mashed potatoes mixed with melted cheese.

Chap did the same. He used to eat a variety, but now all he ate was steak or ham and cheese. I'm not sure what caused the craving and taste changes but they were obvious. As I looked around the chow hall, I saw that not everyone was eating like Chap and I. More people who had gone out with us on patrols had the same things on their plates than did before. I began to wonder if it was the experiences that caused the change, or just being over loaded on patrol all the time. Maybe our bodies required what was in the food we now craved rather than anything else available.

I didn't get too much further into the thought. Chap had finished and was waiting on me to leave. I finished what was left of my steak and decided I was done. He got up to leave and I followed him. As we headed out another round of mortars started landing in the base. We just kept casually walking watching the new Marines ducking for cover like we had done when we first got here. The alarm started going off, but it looked like no more rounds were coming in. We continued walking, trying to bide our time until it was time to leave.

We stopped at the USO to get a few supplies for our trip. Surprisingly enough, they were very well stocked even though we were so far from home. Chap and I went to their tobacco products and bought two cartons of smokes, one for Chap and one for me. Then a few cans of dip to split between the two of us. We couldn't smoke on the planes but we could dip and that was a fair substitute for smoking.

We left the USO and headed to where our convoy that was going to take us back was waiting. I guess Chap figured we could make time go by faster by hanging out there. I could nap all day and all the way home if they would let us.

Other Marines with us must have had the same idea. Several were already sprawled out in several areas sleeping the day away. At this point nothing to me was more comfortable than sitting against something in full gear. It always put me to sleep. I looked around and could tell a lot of people felt the same way. Everyone napping near the convoy was in full gear already asleep.

Chap sat opposite of me and was joined by Jonathan as we were attempting to nap. I couldn't sleep so I motioned for him to come over to my side but he didn't respond. I had been trying to figure out if I had accidentally wronged him in some fashion, but I couldn't think of anything. I decided to take a more aggressive approach and act like I was mad at him to provoke him. I said a few profanities to Jonathan and he replied, "I'm not acting that way to you! You've been avoiding me!" I thought for a moment before speaking, "I'm sorry it seemed like I was avoiding you. I wasn't sure how to go back to the way it was. I tried to find you several times but trying to talk to you felt awkward and I could not think of how to fix it."

Jonathan stood up and came to sit beside me as we talked, "Things won't be the same," He said. "I get that. I'm not stupid. I know what this is all about. Dave was your friend too and I get it. All of you are here because of me! Did you ever think of how that makes me feel? Maybe I needed some time sure but you didn't have to avoid me the rest of the deployment."

Chap broke into the conversation slapping me in the back of the head before saying, "Both of you are hurt, so am I. We are here now, so let's start fresh and move on. I'm not saying forget Dave, I'm saying honor who he was by not forgetting. You, Jonathan, are not responsible for us going, we made a choice and volunteered willingly to come here." Chap turned to me sharply and spoke in a harsh tone, "You better learn to quit being such a hermit. It's hurting Jonathan's girly feelings and making me bored."

Jonathan laughed and punched Chap in the arm as he spoke, "I miss hanging out with you guys. I miss crazy ideas and all the trouble we used to get into. I hate this place. I'm glad we are leaving it, and I am thankful you guys are here with me to make it less of a hell than it could have been.

All of us took a nap after that conversation and didn't wake up until Chap's alarm went off for Dinner Chow. The three of us went to the chow hall to eat. It was more crowded than usual due to the extra Marines who had replaced us being on base. Their uniforms looked so clean and all of them looked so excited and happy to be here. It made me remember us, before we discovered different.

I wanted to stand up and warn them—tell them how much they would grow to hate this place, how it can eat at your soul—but I wouldn't, that would be losing it and I needed to stay in control. They would figure it out on their own soon enough, just like we did. I had filled my plate with the usual steak and potatoes with cheese. Chap had just the steak. I knew he would go up for more. Jonathan however, still ate the same thing. He had a few sandwiches a salad and some soup.

It confounded me, why hadn't he changed? With a confused look on my face as I asked him, "How come you're not eating some sort of meat?" Jonathan just shrugged his shoulders as he spoke, "I guess the same reason as anyone here. They have it available any day and I can eat it whenever I feel like it. I'm just not in the mood for it today I guess." I responded, "I was just curious. I can't seem to get enough meat." Chap butted in, "I find that the meat tends to calm me down." I said, "Really? It doesn't really do that for me I just always want it."

I laughed partially out loud and laughed harder inside. It was good being at the table with my friends talking about things that meant nothing at all. I was tired of being serious and not being able to do the things we did at home. I just wanted to go back to being myself and having fun with my friends when we didn't have to work. It was refreshing to know nothing had really changed between all of us.

The three of us were joking and laughing together like we used to do and then I could see the familiar look Jonathan got in his eyes. I knew right away he thought about the same thing I did at the same moment. Instead of letting the mood go to bad I spoke up, "I wish Dave were here to laugh with us. I'm not sure what you guys have planned when you get back but I was thinking I'm going to make a trip to try and see Dave's parents. I want them to know how brave and selfless their son was, I want them to know that he wasn't forgotten, or left behind. I think they need to be told that."

Chap put his hand on my shoulder as he spoke, "That's one of the best ideas I've ever heard you say." Jonathan responded after, "I agree we can all go together I think it would be better for us and the family if we did it that way." None of us finished eating after our conversation. We just got up and left.

# CHAPTER 11

It was finally time to go home and everyone was loaded up in the convoy. We all seemed excited to be leaving and I have to admit, I was happier than I had been since I got there. Jonathan was whistling 'Old Mac Donald Had a Farm' next to me and Chap was already asleep sitting across from me. The convoy started moving and there was a boom of sound from everyone cheering in excitement. I was nervous about being hit on the way, to come so far just to have home snatched away before I could get there. It was a cruel, ironic joke but we had a decent number of escorts with the convoy and I shook off the negative feeling. I'm going home. We headed out the gates and were on our way. For the first time in a while the plant life around the river by the base actually looked nice again. I was starting to hate this place less and less the further we got from the base.

It didn't take long once we were in the outer village for pot shots to hit the convoy and a few mortar rounds to rain down. A few of the Marines with us started yelling profanities. Then shouting things like, "You never could hit the broad side of a barn!" Or "My three year-old son aims better than that!" Everyone at this point were all making jokes at how pathetic the insurgents were and had been at shooting anything at a distance.

After I had analyzed everything that had happened, the only thing they had done well during the deployment were the booby trapped rooms and a hand full of IED's. The mortars were all luck. Mortars killed people sure, and one even got Dave, but when you looked at how many hit the base it was all luck. Even someone blind can hit a target if you gave them enough rounds.

I decided I had enough of that line of thought. I needed to clear my mind and think like I was at home again. We were out of danger on the main road to the air stip. Helicopters had been patrolling the main road often so there hadn't been activity on it for months. We got to the airstrip and could see it had been attacked earlier. There were fresh impact marks and debris that still hadn't been cleaned up. That must have been when our replacements got here, I figured, or maybe it was after—it looked pretty fresh. It could have happened after or maybe both. It was always hard to tell.

As we went through the airstrip's gate the C-130 was already running and waiting for us. The convoy pulled up behind it and stopped. We all started unloading, lining up, and climbing in. We found ourselves a place to sit. I sat next to Jonathan in the two last seats available in that section. Chap smiled as he came up to us and told the PFC beside me to take a hike as he stole his seat. I smiled at him and spoke, "You're not scared I'll puke on you?" he laughed and replied, "No, I don't want you puking on anyone else." With those comments the PFC didn't seem to mind the seat was stolen any longer and found another seat.

Once every one was loaded up, the C-130 violently shook as its engines revved up for takeoff. The noise was to the point you couldn't even have a conversation. Chap smiled and passed Jonathan and me some earplugs he had brought. He signaled to his head and I figured he was either saying 'I'm smart' or 'I remembered from last time' based on his hand motions. I just gave Chap a thumb's up that I understood his gesture and I put the ear plugs in.

The flight wasn't too long and the C-130 started its landing in Kuwait. I had almost gotten sick again as we started to land. Jonathan, in a panic, snatched the puke bag from Chap and gave it to me and yelled over the engines, "Not this time!" Chap laughed hysterically as he watched to see if I would get sick again. Luckily, I didn't. At least now I knew I got sick flying in C-130's for sure when landing. It struck me as odd that I had never gotten sick flying in any other type of plane before, just this type.

We unloaded from the C-130 and a few Air men escorted us to our temporary living quarters. We were to stay here until our final flights home were ready. Once our gear was at our new bunks, an officer from the Kuwait base came in and spoke, "Listen up Marines, you are to stand by and not leave your quarters until an escort comes to take you to our briefing station." The room was dead silent everyone in our bunk house looked to Chap as if for a response. Chap spoke up, "What's this regarding sir?" The Officer responded, "It's regarding your safety on this base and your instructions on how to act when you land back home." The officer left.

Everyone looked around confused, asking each other questions of why and what had potentially happened to cause this? I looked at Chap and said, "Well obviously someone before us screwed up pretty good on the way back home." Chap chucked and responded, "If I wasn't with you, I would have said I know who caused this mess." I laughed and the three of us lay down to take a nap again. It wasn't long before our escort came to our bunk house to take us to the debriefing room. When we got there the room was pretty full and we had to sit in the back. There was a commanding officer up front. We could tell he was high up in rank but from the distance we couldn't see what his actual rank was.

The commanding officer began to speak, "Welcome Marines. I would like to be one of the first to congratulate you on a successful deployment. Now that you are on our base for a few days I would like to lay down a few ground rules. Break these rules and you will delay your trip home by longer than you could imagine. First rule: you are not to have live ammunition. If you are caught with live ammunition, you will be charged and I will keep you here doing God knows what for a long time. The second rule: I know you just came out of a combat situation and you are

Marines by nature and you love to fight. You WILL NOT fight on my base is this clear?" There was a light rumble of mumbles and a few yes sirs but not everyone answered.

The commanding officer spoke again, "Maybe some of you didn't hear me? I said, IS THAT CLEAR?" This time the room echoed with a loud, "YES SIR." The commanding officer said a few more things but I was already somewhere else in my mind and missed it, but when the video on the screen behind him started playing I was dragged back into reality. It was a video on what to expect when we get home and how to act. It told us to seek help for certain feelings, and how the suicide rate when retuning home was high. Chap poked me during the movie and spoke, "What the hell is this garbage? This makes me want to kill myself just watching. Do they think we're twelve or what?" I responded, "Well so far what I can gather from the video is it looks like someone was forced to make it based on the high number of incidents that have happened once they have gotten home. It was made poorly and not for us as a target audience apparently. It was probably made to make the group that wanted it made happy, that's where they messed up. "Jonathan spoke up, "They mean well at least, they are trying to give us information and help us."

Chap laughed and patted Jonathan and I on the back and said, "You guys analyze things too much." I shrugged and responded as I elbowed Jonathan and smiled, "It's a gift and a curse." By the time we were done talking the video was over and everyone started getting up to leave. Chap spoke as we stood up, "Where's the chow hall in this place? I'm starving." I shrugged my shoulders and kept walking out the door. Jonathan pushed Chap from behind as he spoke, "You're always hungry, fatty." Chap kicked the sand on the floor at Jonathan and replied, "I'm in better shape than both of you." We all laughed as we kept walking.

Once the three of us were outside I said, "Let's walk around and see what is all available to do around here." Chap and

Jonathan followed my lead as I walked toward where most of the buildings were located. We happened to get lucky in the direction I chose to travel. I almost had a heart attack; we could see a coffee shop and a few fast-food places in what looked like a food court no less! Chap started laughing and said, "Now that's something I never thought I'd see in the desert. "I laughed as well and replied, "Too bad we didn't have those commodities on our base." Chap responded, "From what I heard, they were doing the coffee shop there at least. It's always good to know what businesses support their country." I laughed and nodded my head in agreement. Chap and I both stopped at the burger place and Jonathan went to the pizza place. All of us ordered as many items off of the menu that we could carry to the bench. None of us cared how expensive or bad for us the food was. All we cared about was eating junk food and we wanted to have it all!

We sat eating for what felt like several hours. At this point I had already smoked almost half my pack of cigarettes. I discovered that not having anything to do would increase my need to smoke. I hadn't noticed the whole time, but as I sat here watching both my friends, I realized that my hand tremors had been almost nonexistent since we left. Chap seemed more calm and nonaggressive. I began to wonder if Jonathan was having issues like we had been. He seemed perfectly fine to me though looking at him now.

I didn't get to far in thought before Chap slapped me on the back hard and spoke, "Relax why so tense? You're in thought, I can tell. There is nothing that important to think about right now let's just enjoy the limited freedom we have." I smiled and nodded. All of us picked up our trash and threw it in the trash cans. We looked at the signs around us and then headed in the direction to where the recreational building arrow was pointing.

Chap lead the way and Jonathan and I followed. When we got into the recreational building it was a lot bigger than it looked like on the outside. There were foosball tables, pool tables, ping pong tables, a few game consoles, and television theatre room. We all stared in awe. It was more free entertainment than we had seen in our lives!

Despite all the various things to do the three of us agreed we just wanted to play pool. We set up a game of cut-throat and started playing. We continued to play until we were hungry again. We headed back to the food court but time had flown by and it was too late everything was closed. We had spent too many hours in the recreational building playing pool. It was as if that old axiom, 'Time flies when you are having fun' was true.

There were direction sign all around. We found the one that pointed to the chow hall and followed it. Thank goodness it was open and we all let out a sigh of relief. When we got inside it was lot smaller than our other chow hall. I figured most everyone must go to the food court. There were a few people there eating but it was pretty empty. All that was available were a few meats, sandwiches and a variety of fruit.

Chap and I piled on the meat and Jonathan grabbed a few sandwiches and an apple but we didn't spend too much time eating. All three of us finished in less than five minutes and Chap motioned for us to leave. Once we got out of the chow hall the three of us lit a smoke. I looked at my pack which I had just opened this morning and it was empty.

Chap smiled at me as he said, "Flipping your Lucky and smoking it last paid off." He reached into his cargo pocket and tossed me another pack. I smiled and replied, "Thanks, left all mine in the carton at the bunk house. I didn't think I would go through the whole pack." Jonathan asked, "Who do you think came up with flipping the Lucky cigarette and smoking it last?" Chap answered, "Not sure. I don't really believe in it but I've always done it to be on the safe side you never know."

The smoke made us realize we were tired, so we headed back to the bunk house. Once we got there it looked like most everyone else was already asleep. The three of us crawled into our bunks and tried to go to sleep. It was a few hours before Jonathan woke me up. As I looked up at him, I flipped him the bird. He pointed at his eyes and then at Chap. I looked over and Chap had pretty much ripped his pillow to shreds with the knife he carried.

I motioned Jonathan over to me and I crept over to Chap. I had to be careful and get the knife before he swung it. I pointed at Jonathan and then Chaps legs. When Jonathan gave me a thumb's up I knew he was ready whenever I was. I positioned myself in front of the knife and had my other hand ready to cover Chaps mouth so he wouldn't make too much noise.

I was faster than I thought. I had not only gotten the knife out of Chaps hand and dropped it on the floor, but had his head in a decent lock with his mouth covered so he didn't make very much noise. Jonathan had his legs and with all his weight held them in place as Chap struggled. After a few seconds

Chap quit fighting and I knew it was okay to let go he was awake and aware of his surroundings now.

He stood up, composed himself, and started walking out of the bunk house. He never spoke a word, but you could see the fear in his eyes. I picked up the knife and followed him out while Jonathan collected what was left of the pillow and stuffed it in the trash. A few of the other Marines in the room were looking to see who made the noise. It looked as though they were not sure of what had happened. Maybe they knew and were fighting their own battles.

When I got to Chap outside, he had broken down and was on his knees crying. I didn't say anything, I just sat next to him and lit two cigarettes, handing him one. Jonathan came out shortly and sat on the other side of Chap and started smoking as well. I could tell Chap was having a hard time with what had happened. I'm pretty sure he felt like I did with my issues. I thought earlier we might have gotten rid of our problems by leaving, but as I held my smoke to my mouth my hand had already been trembling, I just hadn't noticed till I paid attention to myself.

Chap spoke up as we stared at the stars in the night sky, "Sorry guys, I don't know what's got into me. I can't sleep without my gear and it's not exactly safe for anyone when I do." Jonathan put his arm around Chap and said, "There's nothing to be sorry about. It is what it is. We all have something going on. We just have to find ways to hide it. I spoke up, "I've been hiding my problems for months now." Chap looked over to me and said, "We've all seen your trembling hands. You're no better to wake up sometimes either, you've hit me twice. You just don't carry a knife." I smirked as I spoke, "Yeah I remember seeing you on the floor a time or two. Jonathan spoke up, "This isn't funny." I frowned and replied, "You got to laugh at it or you won't make it."

Chap spoke as he put out his smoke, "Did anyone see?" Jonathan responded, "No.

But you got the mattress, so we need to flip it over." We quietly went back inside and flipped over the mattress. I showed Chap the knife and put it in my pack where he couldn't easily get it. We all tried to get to sleep but Jonathan was the only one that seemed to fall asleep after that.

When morning came around, I could see that Chap hadn't really slept after I took the knife and I stayed awake to guard my pack from him taking it back. Jonathan however was snoring up a storm. Chap woke

Jonathan up and we all got our stuff to go to the showers. From what we heard the showers here were better than anything else we could have hoped for in Iraq. Sure enough there was scalding hot water. I think I must have scrubbed myself clean twice, it felt so good to have an actual decent shower. Once we were done, we did the usual shave, brush teeth, check to see if hair needed to be cut. Then we headed back to the bunk house to put away our bathroom gear.

We headed to the chow hall for breakfast and looked in surprise at all the different countries military forces that were on the base. We ran into a Canadian Sniper, Korean soldiers, British soldiers, a few Australians. It was as if in the morning everyone came out. We didn't see anyone other than the US Army and Marines at night. I wondered what they were all doing here.

I knew they were probably doing the same as we were but where? I have never seen this many different soldiers anywhere. I knew a few back at base in Iraq but only a handful. There were hundreds of people from different countries here.

We headed to the recreational building to play pool again but this time it was packed. There wasn't anything available that didn't have a line to wait in. Jonathan spoke up as we stood by the door way, "Well I don't know about you gents but I don't feel like being in a crowd." Chap responded, "I agree let's just find somewhere to sit out of the sun. Maybe we could check out the shops here."

I followed Chap and Jonathan to all the places they thought they wanted to go. After they bought a few souvenirs and seemed to be content, we headed back to the bunk house. We were leaving tomorrow so we didn't have too much time to wait around anymore. Chap tried to get me to go with him and Jonathan to the recreational building again but I was content sleeping off the rest of my time here. I didn't follow them out of the bunk house.

# CHAPTER 12

I had slept most of our remaining time away. We had already packed and cleaned up the bunk house we were staying in and everyone was waiting to go. A small man in civilian clothing came to our bunk house and said to follow him. We all filed in line walking with him to the buses that were waiting by the dirt road. The buses were comfortable and air-conditioned. Chap secured the back seat of the bus and Jonathan and I sat with him. Once we were all seated the bus pulled away. It went onto a main stretch of highway that had signs above it like they do back home, but it was foreign and I couldn't read anything the signs said.

The bus ride only took a few hours and we were at a civilian airport for our trip home. We had a separate section that we had to go through and the security didn't check anything on us. I figured probably because we were all carrying weapons. Our Ammo had been turned in with any gear we borrowed at the Iraq base. Everyone who wanted anything smuggled put it on the quad cons. So there really wasn't any point for them to check us and they knew it.

Foreign personnel called out our names and handed us a card attached to a lanyard to go around our necks. It had a bar code on it with our pictures. I looked at it and wondered where they got the picture from. Then I recognized that it was the same picture on my military ID. I guess it made sense, but I was uncomfortable with strangers in another country having my picture.

Jonathan pushed me to get my attention and asked, "You bring any dip? We can't smoke in here or on the plane." I lightly laughed and handed him the extra can I packed and told him, "That's the only other can I have. Make it last." He gave me a thumb up as he packed the can and stuck some in his lower lip.

We were escorted through the rest of the airport to the plane terminal. They scanned the cards they gave us as we boarded the plane. A few people who had brought their phones now had them unpacked and were texting on them. They had discovered we had cell reception, much to their delight—if I was reading the look on their faces right.

There were no assigned seats so Chap moved us to the back of the plane and we sat to wait for takeoff. It was really weird seeing so many people with weapons on a civilian plane. It didn't quite feel right, but I shook the feeling off and tried to clear my mind. We were on our way home, this was a time to be happy and excited. For some reason I didn't feel happy, I was feeling anxious and worried. There was no explanation for my feelings, I wanted to feel happy, I should be looking forward to going home, and this made me feel even worse. I tried to relax and stop thinking about it all.

I looked over at Chap and Jonathan. They were already relaxing in their seats and it looked like they were going to nap the on the ride home. I decided that was a good plan and tried to do the same. I tried to rest but I could still hear all the sounds around me and started to get a little frustrated. I sat back up Chap must have already figured out why I was squirming in my seat and handed me a set of ear plugs. I thanked him and attempted to sleep again.

I wasn't asleep long before the noise level on the plane went through the ear plugs. I opened my eyes to see Marines passing around several bottles of alcohol; someone had obviously done well at smuggling. I decided not to think too much on it and joined in the drinking with everyone else. The stewardesses were laughing and mingling with the group. I saw more than once a stewardess and Marine sneaking into the bathroom together.

I decided I was done with the celebration

and headed back to my seat. I noticed Chap hadn't come back to his yet. Jonathan was already sitting down but I could tell he was feeling the alcohol. I sat down and put the ear plugs back in. I watched everyone as they had a good time laughing and talking.

Chap came back and sat in his seat with an obvious grin on his face. I leaned over and could smell the perfume. I pulled one ear plug out and said, "You dirty dog." Chap responded, "I am now! Don't hate. You know you're jealous. I laughed and responded, "If it was that easy you might want to see the doc when you get back." Chap responded, "It wouldn't be anything you haven't got before."

I chuckled as I leaned back into my seat and put my ear plugs back in. Chap was never like that before. I guess people do change, but that still seemed excessive. At least he's enjoying himself, I need to think of something I would enjoy doing when I get back. I couldn't seem to shake this feeling of misery and want to be alone. Chap must have felt it too. He kept pushing us to the back of everything, as far away from everyone that we could physically get, or maybe so he can see everything in front of him and not have to worry about what's behind him. I couldn't tell which one and I did not want to open the subject due to my own issues at the moment.

I let my thoughts fight over why Chap was acting the way he was and I slowly floated into sleep as my thoughts drifted away. I experienced what I thought was my first bad night terror; I wasn't quite aware of my surroundings and saw myself back in Iraq. I was where the wall of the room exploded on Chap and me. I tried to yell at the two Marines in front of me not to go in but it was like they couldn't hear me. I tried to run after them to stop them and the hallway kept getting narrower and narrower, everything in my vision started to stretch out into a tunnel that looked like it never ended. Then suddenly I couldn't move my arms or my legs I tried to scream but nothing came out.

I was shaken awake and was in the middle of the plane aisle and as I became more aware I saw everyone staring at me. Chap helped me up and I quietly walked back to my seat. Good buddy that he is, he yelled, "Mind your own business people! The show's over!" Chap took over the aisle seat and pushed me to the window seat, saying, "Didn't I tell you, you were worse. You've been doing that for the past few months, so much for hiding it, you damn drama queen." I could tell Chap was frustrated. I knew he meant well by what he said so I didn't take it personally. Jonathan, however, must not have and spoke up, "Don't even think of cutting into him after what you pulled the other night Mr. Knife Happy." I started to chuckle as that name had rung pretty true. Jonathan saw I was laughing and relaxed when he realized I wasn't upset. Chap however was now in a bad mood and just put his ear plugs in and tried to sleep the rest of the flight off.

The plane landed in South Carolina. There were a few buses already there waiting for us to get on for the last leg of our trip to Camp Lejeune. Almost all of us dropped to our knees and kissed the ground as we got off the plane. It was the most relaxed feeling I have had in a while.

All of us excitedly packed into the buses. Chap as usual lead Jonathan and me into the back of the bus. The conversations around us all sounded the same. Everyone was talking about going home or hitting the bars and clubs. Most everyone's plan was pretty much to drink themselves stupid.

Jonathan had already fallen asleep; Chap and I carefully pushed him to the window seat so we could talk. Once we sat back down Chap spoke up, "Jonathan wanted us to go to his house for the celebration party his wife was throwing for our return home." I responded, "I don't know, I might show for a bit, it depends. How many people are going to be there?" Chap frowned as he answered, "A lot." "Then I'll show up and make an appearance, but once I've seen him, his wife, and kid, I'll be leaving." I replied.

Chap sat quietly for a moment as if in thought and spoke up, "Things will go back to normal, you'll see. It will be like old times I promise." I replied, "Don't make promises you can't keep. Besides I've never met your family, let alone anyone else's. I like to keep my world small and organized—as far as who I decide I want to know, and spend time with." Chap replied with a harsh tone, "You're full of crap. You haven't always been that way. You used to be overly social. I could go as far as saying you used to talk too much, literally to everyone."

I knew he was exaggerating a bit, but in reflection he was correct. At one time I did talk to everyone. I felt now that person had died a long time ago. Boot Camp had done a good number to kill my old personality, but now the rest of what I had left of who I used to be was dead. I was hiding it from everyone but inside I knew. I wasn't who I once was. The question was: who had I become? I didn't even know myself let alone how to explain it to Chap. I finally just shrugged and said, "I'm not that bad. I just don't feel like being around people I don't know is all."

Chap punched my shoulder then spoke, "I'm interacting with his family. You damn well better be there and stay for a while. You're not leaving me there by myself." I knew Chap was guilt tripping me but he was right. I couldn't leave him there alone now—I had to stay until he was ready to leave. I responded, "Fine. I don't have to behave myself, so if I have a stupid idea for fun, it's happening." Chap just smirked but didn't respond. I guess he was just happy with winning the argument.

The busses pulled into the gates of Camp Lejeune. There was a huge roar of cheers and celebration on the bus. We could see over a hundred people with signs and flags cheering as we pulled into the parking lot. My family was still back home, so I knew there was no one here for me. I could tell

Chap was looking for his Ex but I knew she wouldn't be there either. Jonathan however was awake and yelling at the window now. I could see his family holding up the signs for him screaming and waiving their flags.

Everyone seemed to be in a rush to greet everyone. The last to get off the bus were Chap and I. Neither one of us were in a hurry. Chap looked up to me and said, "Let's go to a bar. We can catch up with Jonathan later. Let his family have some quality time with him. As we walked to our barracks I watched as Jonathan's daughter ran into his arms crying while she yelled 'Daddy! Daddy!' I could see tears of joy in his eyes too. I was glad to see Jonathan smile, he didn't very often and I figured maybe he would now.

As we got to the barracks, I could see my Toyota Celica was still where I had parked it and Chaps old Ford F150 was parked right next to it. I started laughing hysterically as we got closer. Chap spoke, "What is so funny?" I pointed at his tires and continued to laugh.

Two of his tires were flat on the ground. Chap started saying a few profanities then composed himself and spoke, "We can take care of that later. Looks like you're driving."

I set down my gear and pulled a small bag out. Inside it were my keys, wallet and cash I had made while in Iraq. Chap looked at me funny and spoke, "Gamble much do you?" I laughed and responded, "I told you a night on the town on me when we got back remember? This is our budget. Once it's gone, then it's gone. There's almost a thousand dollars here." Chap replied, "Sounds good enough to me. I don't think we'll need that much."

We put our packs in the trunk of my car and got in. I put in the key and turned. Nothing. No lights or sound. This time Chap was laughing and pointing at me. Once he caught his breath Chap spoke, "Serves you right for laughing at me. Taxi?" I lightly laughed at the situation and replied, "Yeah... taxi."

It didn't take long for the taxi to get to us.

They must have known a group got back and planned for it. I did notice a few had been waiting where the bus had parked. Chap and I found one and got in. He spoke to the driver, "To the closest bar with a pool table." Chap then looked at me and said, "Bar hopping?" I answered, "This night is for you." Chap spoke back to the driver, "We are bar hopping tonight. The more bars we go to the bigger the tip. We are spending an hour per bar, maximum. You keep track of the time and get us when the time is up. Keep the meters running until we're back at the barracks."

The taxi driver spoke, "You boys just get back?" I replied, "Yep, and we are out to have a good time." The driver spoke, "I'll give you my welcome home special rate and charge you half for wait time in-between on one condition…" Chap responded, "What condition is that?" The driver spoke, "No fights. It'll ruin your night and I have to come find you for payment. It happens a lot." Chap laughed lightly as he spoke, "You got a deal. No fights then." Chap gave me a glare as to say I better not start one. I lightly laughed and said, "Not tonight I promise."

The taxi drove off. I wasn't sure where he was heading but as he was driving, he was talking about how great the pool tables and drinks were. When we arrived, it didn't look too bad on the outside. One thing I've learned about bars, never judge it by outside. I was all about what was inside and how good the bartender was. We gave the taxi driver one hundred dollars in twenty dollar bills to secure his services and to start our timer.

We walked into the bar. It was quiet, but it was also only around six in the afternoon. It would be this way at any bar until around eight or so. We walked to the bartender and ordered his house special regardless of what it was. Chap ordered six shots of Jaeger bombs. He set two in front of me and two in front of himself. The other two shots he placed in the center of the table.

I saw a tear rolling down his face as he raised his first glass and started speaking, "To those lost, May we never forget." We both took the shot and raised the second. Chap spoke again, "To Brothers who fight and drink together." We took the shot again. This time Chap hesitated before speaking. He grabbed one of the center ones and I did as well. He looked at the glass as he spoke, "These are for Dave. There was no toast. It was obvious Chap wanted to drink the drinks that Dave would have if he were here. I nodded in agreement and took the shots with him.

Chap spoke up as he started racking the pool table, "Enough of all the sappy crap. We're here to have fun." I lit a cigarette as he racked the balls and set up to break. Chap, as always, would win the game most of the time. We played more than a few rounds when the taxi driver came in to get us.

We paid our tab and got into the taxi to head to the next bar and repeated the process a few times. At eight, the bar we were currently at started getting busy. I started to feel uncomfortable and trapped as the bar started to get packed. The noise of everyone talking started echoing in my mind as my brain tried to process every sound. I started getting overwhelmed with all the sensations as my senses were in hyperactive mode as if I was in a combat situation.

Time seemed to slow down and my adrenaline started rushing. I felt as if I was on full alert looking for danger. I knew there was none but my body was telling me otherwise. Chap must have recognized a look in my eyes. He didn't even say anything. He just paid the tab grabbed my arm and took me to the taxi.

Chap looked at me in the taxi and spoke, "That place was getting boring anyways let's go somewhere quiet and finish the night off." I smiled at his understanding and just nodded my head. He talked to the taxi driver for a moment and the driver said, "I know just the place." The taxi drove out of the city limits and to a bar that was located on the beach.

Looking from the outside it looked like it was closed but the driver assured us it was open. Chap gave me a holy crap look as we walked up to the door. When I walked in it was fairly empty. It looked okay from the inside but nothing special stood out. It had a karaoke machine and two pool tables. What really caught my eye was the balcony that looked over the ocean. I looked at Chap with enthusiasm and said, "Let's see how good the drinks are. If they are good this will be my new watering hole." Chap laughed and responded, "Yeah, out dated and run down: just like you."

The bartender was a woman that looked to be in her late thirties. She wasn't exactly 'easy on the eyes' but her voice was soft and her eyes said she had spirit. Chap, same as usual asked for one house special and six shots of what the bartender thought would be the best. It was his way of testing her ability to make drinks. He usually judged on quality and quantity in which they were made. He could always tell if a drink was shorted in alcohol content.

As he sipped the special, to his surprise, she had put in a little extra instead of shorting the drink. He gave me a thumb's up to signal he liked the place. I set up the pool table as he brought the drinks. I wasn't sure what was in those shots but the bartender seemed to be keen on watching us take all six. Chap raised the first glass and said, "Brothers," down it went. I grit my teeth as that actually made me wince when I drank it. Wow, it felt like fire brandy and Bacardi 151 but I wasn't sure.

Chap looked up as he grabbed the second shot and spoke again, "Remember," and down the second shot went. Chap grabbed the third glass and said a few profanities aimed at Dave and down the third shot went. I could feel the three shots kicking in fairly fast. I had to lean against the pool table to maintain my balance. Chap ordered some food and we started our game of pool. I had lost count of how many games I was down. I was getting better as the night progressed however.

After a few hours we found ourselves on the balcony at the back drinking and smoking as we relaxed and watched the waves. Chap put his hand on my shoulder and spoke, "It's good to be home." I smiled but didn't say anything. I was enjoying the sound of the waves crashing on the beach and the quiet of the bar. We were the only two left except for the bartender and taxi cab driver. The taxi cab driver had come in to get us but when we told him this was the last bar. He just sat in the corner and listened to music until we were ready to go. Chap decided it was time to head back and motioned for me to get up and follow him. We paid the tab and gave an overly generous tip to the bartender. The taxi cab driver followed us out to his car and helped us get in. Both Chap and I had stumbled a few times and were pretty loaded at this point.

The drive to the base ended up being a little longer than I had planned. I felt myself getting sick as we drove and told the driver to pull over. Chap held me out the door by my shirt as I puked all over the pavement. As I puked I could hear the taxi driver lightly laughing. I puked a few more times before we got back to the barracks.

The taxi cab driver, even after getting our payment and good tip, still escorted us to our barracks rooms and opened the doors for us as well. He gave Chap a few of his cards and thanked us for the entertaining night and left. Chap couldn't get me on my bunk so he left me on the floor. As Chap tried to climb up to his bunk he fell on the floor as well. He said a few profanities and just pulled the sheets off the bed and onto himself. I tried to laugh at him but I still felt a little sick as every time I closed my eyes, the world spun in circles. I'm not sure how long I could fight the feeling before I had to puke again. I closed my eyes and slowly the spinning stopped and I passed out.

# CHAPTER 13

Chap and I had been going to the bar on the beach regularly, every night, for a quite a few days. Jonathan had joined us a few times and brought poker cards when he came. We fell into a nice routine of shots and drinks when we were off work.

This whole week had been nothing except classes of how to act in public and around civilians after our deployment. We weren't allowed to go on leave until the classes were finished. A small annoyance, but at least we weren't working hard. The hard part was staying awake during the classes. Soon as class was over it was straight to the bar.

We had been drinking too much to drive so we kept using the same taxi. He would drop us off at the bar at five and pick us up at one thirty before last call. We had gone through all my extra money but I still had six months' pay left. I figured I would last a while. Chap and I seemed to get more comfortable as we got into a routine. All our uniforms were in the exact order. Everything had a place. We did PFT with our squads every other day and went to class. After class, it was off to the bar, then from the bar to pass out in our room at the barracks.

We had a routine. I felt normal again, for once. The routine would have to end though. I had to go see my family, and Chap to see his. I planned it out. I had an eight hour drive home, would be home for almost thirty days, then I would do a detour to drive back and see Dave's family and meet Chap and Jonathan there. I figured it was simple enough. I gave myself two days to get back just in case something went wrong.

We were in final formation and our commanding officer was giving us a release speech. He stood straight and firm in front of us with a slight frown and spoke with a stern deep voice. "On your leave: those of you not married will treat women with respect and at least give them a second date before bedding them." A few snickers and laughs ran down the ranks. He spoke again, "Those that are married: if I hear you beat your wife or your kid I will tear you apart myself. Is that clear?" A loud ringing in tune "YES SIR!" followed.

He looked at everyone up and down before spoke again, "If you fight and I have to bail you out, you will pay for it. There will be NO drinking and driving. You will not drive like an idiot and kill yourself. Is that clear?" Another loud ringing "YES SIR!" He continued, "There have been a lot of incidents in several other companies since we have been back I do not want to hear that any of those things has happened to you. Dismissed!"

As we prepared to leave, Chap, Jonathan and I shook hands and parted ways. Jonathan was staying home here on base with his wife and kid. Chap was going to see his family like I was, and then we both were heading to see Dave's parents on our way back.

I started what I knew was going to be a long drive. My first stop off-base was the local gas station right out of the main gate. I then got on the highway and started driving. I rolled through the radio trying to find a decent country station and finally found one. I was lucky with my car. Jonathan replaced the battery for me and it was running. It had been sitting too long and died. Chap however, had to get four new tires after someone had apparently slashed them. Whoever did must have been the one that keyed his truck too. I'm not sure who he pissed off.

I brushed my distracting thoughts away and focused on the road. It had been six months since I had to follow road signs but it was like riding a bicycle—you never really forget how to do it. You just have to get back in practice.

A few hours into my drive I wasn't paying attention I saw flashing lights in my mirror and heard the siren. I looked at my speed I was going twenty over. I said a few profanities and called myself an idiot as I pulled over.

The State patrol Officer came to my door and asked for my license and registration just like in the movies. I had grabbed both my military ID and license with registration and added my insurance to it just in case as I handed it all to him.

As he reviewed everything, I handed him he asked, "What's the hurry son?" I replied, "To be honest, I wasn't paying attention. First time driving in a while, just got back from Iraq." The Officer handed me back all my papers and ID's and said, "Thank you for your service son. I'll tell you what: I'll let you go on one condition. You don't speed the rest of your trip and you drive safe." I chuckled and replied, "I can do that." The Officer shook my hand and sent me on my way.

The rest of the drive was pretty uneventful. I stopped every two hours to get out stretch and then get continued driving. After almost nine hours I could see the turn off to my grandparents' house where everyone was there waiting for me. The drive took a little longer than I expected, but a few of my injuries had acted up along the drive. So I had to pull over more often than I thought I was going to.

It was dark outside but I could see the lights in the house were on and the yard was full of vehicles. When I opened the door to greet everyone I was surrounded with hugs and family. My grandparents still had food set out for me from my long drive. It was of course a list of all my favorites.

I sat at the table as everyone took turns patting me on the back and still greeting me telling me how great it was to have me back home. Everything looked just like I remembered nothing changed. For a moment I felt a comfort like a little child in a mother or father's arms.

I started eating the food and sampling as much as I could. Nothing tasted like I remembered. I knew they made it the same but something about my taste had changed. The only thing that didn't was oyster stew.

When I got to it, and experienced the taste in my mouth my face lit up like a Christmas tree. This was familiar, this was comfort and memories, and this was indeed my favorite.

I was no longer sad to see the rest of my favorites go. I still had my love of soup, especially this soup. Food was a comfort to me and I fixated on how good the oyster stew made me feel. I now had more reasons than taste to love it so much. I had worried so much about my tastes changing but this, at least, was the way I remembered and enjoyed it.

My family could see I was content and happy with the food they had left for me and stayed up for a while to talk. After I had my fill of the soup, we put all the remaining food away for later and set off to bed. I slept in what used to be my mother's room when she grew up. There was a painting she did when she was younger, hanging above the bed.

I had slept in that room many times before when I was growing up and visiting. When

I woke, I tried to be quiet as to not wake everyone it was about five in the morning. When I got in the living room my grandfather was already sitting in the chair watching the news with the fireplace going. I smiled as I greeted him and sat in the chair next to him.

He didn't say much as we sat there; a few comments about what was on the news here or there. I could tell he was trying to make simple conversation and was deliberately avoiding the deployment topic. I knew he meant well, but I could tell he was trying to get me to lead the conversation. I just wasn't up to it.

It didn't take long for the rest of my family to get up and hug and greet me once more. Once there were enough people up my Grandfather started making his famous crepe pancakes. I had attempted the recipe a few times myself but even following Grandpa's directions, it never was even close.

Grandpa wanted me to be the first to have one since it had been so long. They tasted like I remembered—another favorite saved on my list. Maybe things weren't so different. I felt a little tingly in the face and lightly on edge but normal with everything else.

Once breakfast was over, everyone started cleaning up and we headed out on the property. Grandpa had lots of beautiful property to wander around on. It was one of my favorite things to do at their house. We got on his home-made vehicle that was a cross between a small tractor, a golf cart, and a go cart all in one. Everyone had nick named it 'fliver'.

I drove the fliver around the property until it was almost out of gas. When I got back Grandpa asked questions about what I thought of his new modifications and how she handled. I could do nothing except give him praise about it. His work was always something to be respected and admired.

I went out shooting the guns with my dad and brothers. I had shown my brothers the proper use of the rifle strap to give you better aim, how to steady your shot in multiple positions, fast reloading techniques, and shoot and movement. They seemed excited and impressed with each thing I showed them.

My father was just relaxing, watching us do everything. Every now and then one of my brothers would ask him to try but he would just say he's having just as much fun watching. I was enjoying my time with the family everything felt and seemed like it should be.

As we walked down the path a few questions came up I knew were going to be asked eventually. Did you kill anyone? What was it like over there? What did you do there? Did you get shot at? Every question I almost felt myself flinching just hearing it.

I gave vague and non-descriptive answers and kept trying to change the subject. What I couldn't understand was what is going on in my head. Why am I getting defensive? I felt like I had pins stabbing the skin on my face as

I tried to control my thoughts and reactions to their questions.

These were all innocent enough questions for anyone to ask, but my mind felt like I was under attack. I tried to fight the feelings but the more I fought the angrier I became. The one thing everyone kept saying that almost set me on fire was: 'I understand' and 'Everything is going to be fine'.

I had to find a way to avoid this. I just wanted normal time with my family. I wanted to enjoy myself. I found myself disappearing in enough small increments that my family didn't really notice. It gave me enough time to collect my thoughts and come back and act normal.

I knew nothing they were doing was wrong. I would have asked and done all the things they did. I had to take a breath, calm myself down and just deflect the question, change the subject, or give vague answers. Once I had my strategy on how to handle everyone, everything seemed to go back to normal.

The questions slowly stopped and everyone went back to the way it was.

After a few days in, I went out fishing with my uncle. It had been a long time since I had been fishing. I remember as a child I would get up way before the sun just to fish with him. My uncle knew all the best spots. We sat in the boat fishing for hours. The best part was we just relaxed. Had one beer or two and fished all day. It was like he knew what I needed and if I wanted to talk I would. We talked about food, things I like, fishing. Mostly we just enjoyed each other's company and just fished. I enjoyed every moment I spent with my family. There were a few awkward moments but when my family got off the topic of Iraq everything seemed normal. I greeted my nieces and gave them all my going away gift necklaces I has acquired while overseas. I gave everyone either hugs, kisses or handshakes good bye.

My family was sad to see me go, but understood. I still had to make the trip to

Dave's house. I turned on my phone when I got to the first gas station to gas up and noticed I had more than a dozen missed calls from Chap. There were no real messages left from anyone, but it was apparent I needed to call someone soon.

I figured it must be important so I called Chap to see what had happened. After talking to him, I sat on the hood of my car for a moment to get a feel on what had happened. Chap had told me Jonathan had shot himself. Something had apparently gone on in the house for his wife to call the MP's and instead of surrendering his weapon, he killed himself.

I felt weak in my knees and almost wanted to throw up. I got up to walk to the door of the car and almost collapsed. I know had tears running down my face and a swirl of emotions in my mind. 'Why would he do that?' I kept asking myself. He was fine when I left. He seemed so happy with his family. I never went to see his family. A thousand thought raced through my mind.

As I sat in my car my hands were still shaking on the steering wheel. I texted Chap because I was no longer in the mood to talk. I wouldn't be going to Dave's parents any more. I could barely control myself now, let alone in front of Dave's family. Chap texted back saying that he agreed and was just going to a bar to think things over. I didn't respond I just started driving.

I found myself in North Carolina by the time I stopped driving. I decided to go to the regular bar I had been going to since we got back. I still had two days to kill so I figured I would just rent the hotel across from the bar or sleep in my car.

The bar tender was observant enough that she didn't bother me other than to fill my drink. She could tell something was wrong and just made a side comment that she was there if I wanted to talk. I didn't want to talk I just wanted my old friend 'double Jack-and Coke'. I didn't need anything else. As I had more to drink than my body could process I could barely stand on my own. The bartender cut me off a while back but I had a flask in my back pocket I had filled before coming into the bar. I kept taking drinks from it as I went to the bathroom.

I found myself playing a four man poker game. I had Chap, Dave, Jonathan and myself. Only I was the only one actually playing. I would start saying profanities to Jonathan as if he were there and yelling at Dave too. Then I would tell Chap to 'mind his own business, I'm not starting trouble' as if they were all talking to me. I think the only reason I didn't get kicked out is the bartender grew fond of us as we all had been coming in. That and the fact I was the only one there tonight.

As I tried to get up to leave I fell and practically flipped the table. The bartender said she was closing anyways and helped me out side. She dug in my pocket and grabbed my room key to the hotel. Took me to my room and even put me in the bed. I passed out as she sat in the chair watching me.

# CHAPTER 14

It had been a while since Jonathan had passed away. I found myself thinking about it several times a week. I didn't know what was going through my friends mind at the time. I could only guess, what I had come to decide on my own, was that the Demon got him. I could imagine what he felt was close to what I was experiencing now.

It's like a nightmare, but you fight it on a daily basis. It starts like this: You're running down a hallway, but it's long and never ending. You have to get to the end, but you don't know why. You start running to get to the end even though it looks endless. All of the sudden you decide I'm tired of running I'm never going to get to the end anyway.

That's when he shows up. The Demon. He's laughing at your failure and starts to chase you. You run as fast as you can but it is never enough. When the Demon catches you he plays with your mind and your senses. You start experiencing a flash back, or you're having a night terror. In the end it doesn't matter what you did, two facts remain: things that aren't real become real to you, and no one around you understands or knows what going on.

Your memory attacks you and your mind is not your own. You do and feel things that betray who you are. You fight The Demon but fighting it only causes you to lose more control. You feel betrayed, angry, confused, lost, helpless, rage, depressed, and then you are numb to all feeling except the anger and rage. All of this in happens in one short moment. It causes you to lash out and fight anything or anyone. You have no sympathy, no regret, and no love. There is only anger, hatred, and rage. Then it's over. You gain some control. You start to be aware of your surroundings. Then a fear hits your gut as you start to realize what you have just done. You frantically search and observe everything in the area. Who did I hurt? What did I do or say?

A few times no one had noticed and it was okay. A few times it was a friend or family member around and they say those words that tear into your mind. "It will be ok, I understand." Those simple words tear a hole in what used to be a good relationship with who ever said it. It could be mother, father, brother, best friend from before the military. Those simple words tore whatever belief in your mind that they could ever help you.

Then there are the bad scenarios. You lash out physically or mentally causing damage to someone you love. It is the ones you hold most dear that will bear the most pain and suffering from what you are experiencing. They say they understand, but they don't. The more they push or try to talk about it, the worse they make the situation. In your mind you want them to be innocent and safe. When they try to invade that part of your life and memories, they start to become tainted.

Your feelings for them get caught in a cross fire of every emotion possible.

The moment stops and I wake up. I thank God it was only another night terror. There's a bang on my barracks door. I open it and it's a lance corporal on duty, watching over the barracks to insure everything is ok. I tell him I'm fine and I apologize for making so much noise. We had been doing a lot of training lately. There was PT every other day at six in the morning. Then breakfast. Then we would do a class or practice drills. Next, we would go to the gun park and check gear or go to the armory and clean weapons. Every now and then we did hand to hand combat practice. By this time the day was over and I would head to my hiding spot to drink the night away.

These days repeated themselves so much I lost track of time. Chap and I no longer played games or did anything that wasn't going to the bar and drinking. It finally got to the point where Chap and I couldn't afford to go to the bar. I hit a low and kept buying the liter bottles of the cheapest vodka at the USO on base. It tasted horrible but it did the job well.

I started drowning myself in alcohol every time I got a chance. I got pulled aside a few times for being drunk in the morning while we were doing PT, usually from drinking so much that my body couldn't physically get rid of how much I had. By the time we ran three to five miles, along with whatever other exercises were thrown in, I had sobered up and was left alone. I knew I couldn't do this forever. Then a way out showed itself, a good friend of Chap was in need of assistance. He had never been to Iraq before and had a family. Chap had left me a note explaining that he had volunteered to go on the deployment and suggest/told my name while he was at it. He knew I wouldn't turn it down if he was going. I felt saved. At last, I could leave this new hell that had created itself.

Over there I would be occupied and busy. There wouldn't be the mundane life of pointless drills and training that never got you ready for battle. It was all a dog and pony show. I would transfer to a unit that would actually be doing something. Would be practicing what came natural to me now. My life could mean something again. I leapt for joy and it was as if a burden was lifted off my shoulders if only for a moment. I had to clean myself up. It was time to hit the gym and be a super Marine again. One of those Marines that everyone says there goes Motto. It was the only way to save me from myself.

It didn't take long for the transfer to go through. Chap had made sure we were bunk mates and had the same room together. By this point I had been going to the gym three times a day and had almost quit drinking. You never truly quit drinking in the Marines— there are moments when it's almost required to bond with your new squad or teammates.

I felt a second wind and was renewed. The flashbacks and night terrors had all but stopped. They still hit but it was so few and far between everyone who notice had just thought it was my Motto kicking in.

I had met Joker a few times. Chap and Joker went to MOS school together. Chap had promised he would keep Joker safe and was obligated to go on the deployment with him. I was obligated to go because Chap was going. It was a sense of duty and honor to protect your battle buddies, even at the cost of your own life. I knew what I was getting into this time around. The best outcome in my mind at this point was to die saving my fellow battle buddies, or go down in a fight taking as many enemies with me I could.

I no longer feared death. I searched for it and this would give me an opportunity to find the worthy death I was seeking. No one, not even Chap, knew at this point I had tried to kill myself twice with alcohol abuse and pills. My body seemed determined not to let me go. This seemed a lot better option than the latter. As much as Iraq felt like hell, at least there I didn't have to worry about my mind making hell where ever I walked.

Chap and I now had a new drinking partner and friend in Joker. I learned real fast why Chap liked him so much. He was fun and had a great sense of humor. It was a nice change to the routine we used to have being just Chap and me.

Joker was married and had a kid. He lived on base housing with his wife and son. The way he worked on vehicles reminded me of Jonathan. It was almost as if I bonded instantly with him and he fit right into our group.

All of us weren't together in squads anymore. I had my own with my new promotion. Chap and Joker had their own as well. We trained our troops hard. We wanted to insure they were prepared for what we were going into. A lot of Marines were relying on our previous experiences to better prepare them. Only a few in the group had been there before.

It was almost better going the second time. I didn't have nerves to shake or worries. I knew I could die and welcomed it. The first time I feared death, I just wanted to be brave. This time around I knew I was no hero. I didn't like being called a hero. I refused to get any medals and submitted no paper work for any awards.

What we did was a job and we did it well. I wanted no part of recognition. My family and friends who had never been couldn't understand that. Most everyone that had been avoided the awards or anything to do with it. There were a few glory seekers and spotlight Marines that wanted them to flaunt or show off. But most of us didn't want to disgrace the true Marines that earn it or paid with their lives for it. True or not, that is how all of us felt.

Training went fast. We were busy and occupied and time seemed to fly by. I had cut my drinking to weekends only. My squad and I were all hitting the gym three times a day. Training was about strength first, then endurance. You didn't need to be the fastest runner. You did need to go a long time with a lot of weight. Weapon, ammo, water, body armor, and gear are not light. Add the fact of carrying it a few miles to the equation—that is what we were preparing for.

We practiced combat training for house-to-house and on a range for long distance shots. You were either good at it or you weren't. Most Marines were decent at it and a few more excelled at it so much that they made up for the very few that struggled.

Time was coming close to what I figured would be my last deployment. Either I was getting out of the Marine Corps with an honorable discharge or I would die with my friends. I knew I wouldn't make it out of the Marines. No one would hire me—I had too many issues. I wouldn't be able to hold a job. Too many of my superiors were concerned with my sanity and I couldn't move up any further than I had. They respected my ability, but were concerned with my previous excessive drinking. My previous superiors had warned them about how bad I had gotten after they got rid of me. They must have been excited when I transferred.

I wasn't exactly the exemplary Marine they wanted to have for looking pretty in a dog-and-pony show. I was about getting the job done and done well. When it came to spit shine me for someone to just come down and see how good we looked lined up and in uniform, I didn't exactly pass inspection with the vodka on my breath. I had dark circles under my eyes from exhaustion and lack of sleep. It almost looked like I had two black eyes.

That was the old pathetic Marine I was. Now I had a renewed sense of duty. I needed to be at my best for my peers. I refused to be the one that let everyone down. Combat ready is what I did and knew. Not the old dog-and-pony show. The difference in how you were treated when you were going to combat and when you were just sitting on your butt was night and day.

It was way better for my issues and morale in a unit getting ready for combat, than being on one that wasn't. Everyone was more understanding. You got pushed hard to perform well. As long as you performed to standard or better, no one messed with you. The better you performed, the more Marines wanted to learn from you and be around you.

The training starts to build bonds with you and your squad that were not possible before. My brain had built walls to keep from being attached. But the way we trained, I couldn't help but respect and admire my fellow Marines. I was built new again and would defend my squad and my buddy Chap with my life.

We trained up until we had to be deployed. My family was still supportive and had driven up to see me off this time around. I said my goodbyes but they didn't know I had not planned to return back home. This tour was supposed to be worse than the last. We were stationed on a different base doing some similar things but mostly on EOD and patrol this time around. This time we were told there would only be danger for those going outside the wire.

Time seemed to fly by. It was as if somebody had the clock on fast forward. I don't know if it was the training or my memory. I stopped having flashbacks and night terrors, but my memory started getting fuzzy. It got to the point I almost couldn't remember anything that had happened my first time in Iraq.

Before I knew it, I was stepping off the airplane in Kuwait again. I had almost forgotten how the hot air would almost rob your lungs of breathable air as I tried to breathe in. The base here hadn't changed. It looked like just the people did. We weren't in Kuwait long. After two days we headed back into Iraq in a C-130 again. But that is a story for another time and for my other book….

# GLOSSARY

**C-130** - Heavy transport plane.

**MOS-** Trade label for what you did in the military.

**USO -** Military version of a convenience store.

**M249 SAW-** Light machine gun that carries 200 round magazines.

**IED -** Improvised explosive device, anything that was used to make a bomb.

**EOD-** A team that goes out and disables IED's.

**Dip-** Tobacco you put in your lip and let it soak. You absorb the nicotine through the skin.

**MRE-** Meal Ready to Eat, Super concentrated food that lasts a really long time and if consumed too much can ruin your digestion.

**HMMV-** is a hummer H1 model military style. Armored on doors and windows is weak underneath and on the roof.

**7 Ton-** Is a rally big troop transport vehicle. No armor for troops carried in the back however.

**Mortar-** An infantry used shell for medium distant targets kill radius range of approximately ten feet depending on the round used.

**Bunk-** Where you slept and kept your belongings.

**Bunk house-** where two or more of you kept your Bunks, could be a shack or better.

**Mosque-** Religious prayer building Muslims pray in.

**Chow hall-** Where we eat.

**On post-** this is used to describe when you are guarding a position usually in a tower.

**On duty-** used to described when you are guarding a barracks or equipment.

**Devil pup-** a term used for someone who is new or fresh to a situation or the Marine corps.139

**Gear-** what you kept with you to keep you ready for any situation.

**M16A2-** Semi automatic rifle, every Marine has one.

**1911 .45-** An older model hand gun that packs more than the average punch.

**M240-** Heavy machine gun.

**AK47-** light machine gun.

**Kevlar plate-** Armor used to protect your front and back from harm.

**Salt dog-** A Marine who has been through something rough at some point in his career, if not multiple times.

**HQ-** The place in which orders came down from sometimes this was not your own command sometimes it was.

**Insurgent-** Terrorist fighting to cause fear in any way they can. Their goal is to inflict as many casualties as possible even at the cost of their own death.

# IN ACKNOWLEDGEMENT

Mom and Dad. You have been the building block of support when I was at my lowest point. The values that you raised me with helped not only carry me through the deployment, but through life as well. Thomas Bailey. You have and always have been a brother to me. Your support and forcing me to be social when I was down carried me through tough times. I wouldn't have done the deployments without you. P.S. I still hate racket ball by the way. R.I.P Thomas Bagosy. This credit is in honor of your memory. You were a great and loyal friend. You commanded respect from those you were around. May your sacrifice be honored and not forgotten. To Mr. Bags. Thank you for everything.

To my loving wife. I don't know how you put up with my daily issues and struggles. Most of the time; I'm a wreck at home. You are my best friend and I hope this book can bring more understanding of why I am and my Battle buddies are the way we are. I owe you my life. You came and saved me when I was in the darkest place and you refused to give up on me. For that you have my everlasting thanks and love. I love you more than you could ever know. To my daughter. When you are old enough to read and understand these words. I hope you know that you are the light I chase after at the end of my tunnel, now that you're in my life. You carry me through and have helped more than you can know. I love you with all my heart.

To Maureen and John. I'm sorry I'm so stubborn and a jerk sometimes. You guys are second parents to me. I appreciate everything you guys do for me. I know it doesn't feel like it or I don't say it sometimes. But I can't change who I am. I can write it down and you can be satisfied by reading it. Lots of love and care.

To my Mema and Papa. You guys are the point of support and love you could only find in fairy tales only I have you in real life. I love and miss you guys a lot and am sorry it is so hard to visit sometimes. To Uncle Herbie- thanks for listening and having those long talks with me fishing. Listening and not judging was what I needed and you did just that. You have been a great role model in my life and I love you and won't forget any of our trips.

Special thanks to Colin V B for reviewing my chapters and giving a good friends support. Special Thanks to My Uncle Jeff, you not only pulled me out of a pinch in finishing the book but are a great support. I also would like to thank my fellow Marines which did not want to be named. Thanks for your support and for sharing your stories. Putting your experience with mine and others has put a lot of pieces back together for me and helped on my ups and downs. Always remember I will always listen that is what helps the most.

This book was written from true stories from multiple marines serving in Iraq from 2003 to 2007, Locations include- Ramadi, Fallujah, Camp Blue Diamond, and several outlying outposts. No single character in the book is one specific individual the stories and locations are deliberately mixed to protect the identities of those they belong to including myself the author.

© 2014, George Adam Day. Except as provided by the Copyright Act March 5, 2014 no part of this publication may be reproduced, stored in a retrieval system or transmitted in any form or by any means without the prior written permission of the publisher.

*Demeter North*

www.ingramcontent.com/pod-product-compliance
Lightning Source LLC
LaVergne TN
LVHW050022080526
838202LV00069B/6889